EASY
STRESS
SOLUTIONS

How to Meditate Like a Master, Banish Anxiety, and Kick Depression to the Curb

Shanna Warner

"When at some point in our lives we meet with a real tragedy – which could happen to any one of us – we can react in two ways. Obviously, we can lose hope, let ourselves slip into discouragement, into alcohol, drugs, and unending sadness. Or else we can wake ourselves up, discover in ourselves an energy that was hidden there, and act with more clarity, more force."

- HIS HOLINESS, THE 14TH DALAI LAMA

Thank you to His Holiness for graciously
giving me permission to quote him.
He is a big fan of meditation, too.

Visit the author's website at
www.ShannaWarner.com.
Published by Manna Services Group, LLC
ISBN

978-1-953098-03-0

This book is dedicated to YOU, dear reader.

For every child who was molested or abused, for every young person who has been raped, for every mother who watches her child slowly dying, for every spouse choosing life over abuse, for every person struggling with the vagaries of fate - you were in my heart as I wrote this book. My deepest desire is for you to find and know personal peace.

Legal declaration: This book was published with the intent to provide beneficial, accurate, and reliable information. When you read it, you acknowledge that both the publisher and author are not experts on the topics covered and all the recommendations are for informational purposes only. Any action you choose to take because of reading this book is at your own risk. The publisher and author have no legal responsibility for any action you take or reaction you might have from any of the practices discussed in the book. Always seek advice from a professional before undertaking any of the actions discussed or before making major changes in your life. Transmission, duplication or reproduction of any part of this book in any format is considered illegal without the express written consent of the author.

INTRODUCTION

"Every day is a new beginning. And each minute
of that day is an opportunity to change your
world!"

EVERYDAY STRESSES LIKE a rude co-worker,
traffic slowdowns, or coffee spilled on your shirt, can
cause short-term stress reactions like headaches or an
upset stomach. I will show you some simple skills to
cope with the regular stresses of life.

But the stress that comes from trauma can be
long-lasting, sometimes for decades. It can limit your
daily ability to function. That type of pain can survive
deep inside your mind and your psyche. Physical
violence often leaves scars, but so does emotional

violence. People who have experienced trauma and tremendous pain can also develop tremendous strength and depth. I will show you the simple skills I use to cope with trauma stress!

Trauma experiences can stay with you, but they do not have to negatively affect your life on an everyday basis. You need positive coping skills that really work. Here is the main goal we are working on in this book: *learning to react less to stress and have more peace!* How do you do that? By uncovering and unlearning the negatives in our life, and then creating better ways forward into a brighter future.

A stressed-out person, affected by repeated emotional and psychological pain truly can become a person filled with peace, happiness and love. I know, because that person is ME. I will show you how I do it. I work on it every day. (The steps I take are easy and free, by the way.)

Managing stress is a life-long process! You will not wake up one day after reading this book and shout,

"Eureka, I'm over it!" Instead, this book is about developing new skills and having the daily determination to live your best life.

Even now, 30+ years after surviving an assault in college, I still have issues when someone walks up from behind. That heightened awareness of "other" behind me is now a permanent part of my psyche. It is a part of my past. I cannot change the past, neither can you. We can only work on the present. Now I have all sorts of helpful skills to deal with my past, present and future!

I developed this book to show you how you can create more peace and happiness in your life. You can change your thoughts, change your focus and retrain your mind.

Strength, beauty, and knowledge can come from the worst experiences of life. Some people collapse and some rise. The difference is in the ability to find that little something inside you that refuses to give up, the will to create a positive life no matter what the circumstances. You can take your stress and suffering, turn it around, and help change your life for the better.

How can you make those changes? It sounds like a huge challenge, and some days you probably just want to give up. I understand. I have been at the point of giving up, too. I know this sounds hard. But the secret is to take small, easy steps every day. Transformation is worth it! Those small steps lead to less stress and more peace.

So, we will start small. The goal is to uncover and unlearn the negatives ideas or habits you have. Work on one or two little things first. Then you get to recreate a happier and more fulfilling pathway! Creating success in one area of your life leads to creating success in other areas.

I have been working on the process of managing stress and healing myself for more than 30 years. I work on myself daily. So please do not think that you are failing because you are struggling, or depressed, or in pain. The fact that you want more peace and happiness shows that you are headed in the right direction.

You are here, right now with me, reading this book, so I know you have the desire to manage it all, to reduce the stress and live a happier life. It is okay if it feels overwhelming or just too hard. Just know that you CAN do this. When you are ready - and you are because you are reading this right now – just know that you CAN!

I will share with you the best tips, tools, and techniques I know. Some of the skills in this book absolutely will work for you. Some of them might not. Keep trying until you find the things that do help. Never give up.

We will start with two of my favorite stress-relieving skills. You can successfully start them today. And they work IMMEDIATELY! They are simple yet profoundly beneficial. You could read the very first chapter, put the book down, never read another word of it, and that chapter would be enough to help you make your life better right then.

Of course, I recommend that you keep reading and keep practicing all the new skills you will learn. This will help you get the maximum impact to reduce as much stress as possible, because this little book is loaded with ideas to help you. You will find suggestions to deal with stress from anxiety, panic attacks, depression, sleep issues, negative self-talk, negative people, and much more!

I am not a therapist, psychologist or psychiatrist. I am a trauma survivor with some seriously beneficial skills to share with you. I always recommend that you seek professional guidance when dealing with stress from trauma. If you go see a therapist, take this book with you and show them what you are doing!

Part of the daily healing process is taking care of both your body and brain. They work together. Your brain is another body part. People will go to the gym and focus on having a strong body and yet never once work on the body parts above the neck!

I get up and exercise because I know it helps. Do I like it? No, not usually. I am a big girl; I struggle with my weight. So, I know it is good for me. I also take really good supplements, along with eating healthy food so that I can fuel my body. I practice mindfulness, relaxation and meditation to keep my mind and brain healthy. AND, I believe in keeping kind, uplifting, supportive people around me. That feeds my spirit! Feed your brain, body, mind and spirit with the best that you can.

You can read this book in any order that you want. You do not have to start with the first chapter. If you find that negative thoughts and anger are creeping up into your mind every day, then start with chapters 14 or 16. If your stress is causing sleep issues, then start with chapters 10 and 11. If you want some quick, easy and fun activities, then start with chapter 15.   Chapters 1-5 will give you some detailed information about what I believe is the most important skill you need in the battle against stress.

There will be chapters in the latter part of the book where you will need to grab a pen and a notebook. A huge part of managing and healing the pain of stress is DOING something about it. So, get a notebook and get ready. Chapters 17, 18 and 19 will take you into the process of transformation. You get the chance to really work on some deep issues.

As you change old skills by learning new skills, you will find some come easier to you and some are harder. Do not let a difficult section of the book slow you down. Just skip it and come back to it later. Focus instead on the parts of the book that do work for you, that help you feel better, and help you find more peace!

Just remember that the hard things you face can often teach you the most. In a few weeks come back and read this book again. You just might find something else that brings some relief. And that is exactly what I want for you! To help you keep up with the content in the book, at the end of each chapter there is a list of the ideas and themes for that chapter. It is a little shortcut for you to find the tools, tips, and techniques that will help you.

As we go through this book together, I will share some stories from my life. Do not waste one single moment of your time feeling sad or bad for me. Those stories are there to inspire you! I want you to know that you can rise up, no matter how badly life stomps you down, no matter what kind of stress you are dealing with, no matter what you have lived through.

There is only one "rule" I want you to follow as you read this book and as you work through the chapters: BE KIND TO YOURSELF. Be patient about the changes you are making. Transformation does not happen overnight. Take it one day at a time. It is easier for me now and it will get easier for you, too.

You CAN do this. You are stronger than you can imagine. You have incredible resources down deep inside that you can access. Life is more manageable when you find and develop that inner strength. So, get ready. Are you?

Good. Here we go.

CHAPTER 1: MY TWO MOST BENEFICIAL TOOLS

"We all know that exercise is good for the body. But did you know that meditation is exercise for your soul?"

MY TWO MOST BENEFICIAL TOOLS are easy to use and free! I have used them to change my life in the battle against stress, depression, anxiety, nightmares, panic attacks and PTSD. You do not need any expensive gadgets or an expensive education. They are: Exercise and Meditation.

Exercise has increased my physical strength and stamina; meditation has increased my mental strength and stamina. If you accept the idea that you have an inner divine nature, a soul or a spirit, then please understand that it needs to be cared for much like the physical body does. Both the outer and the inner body need tender, loving care.

The inner "you" is untouchable, invisible, and unique. All of the feelings, ideas, emotions and reactions you have are part of that inner body. The inner you IS the real you. Meditation can be a part of taking care of the real you!

I credit meditation with saving my mental and physical life! Please read that last statement again. I will share a few personal stories as we go along in this book together that will help you understand WHY and HOW it helped.

Meditation is both easy and hard. I know that sounds a bit confusing. It is easy to do once you learn the basics. You will learn enough about meditation that you can begin immediately today. When you can make your mind quiet and can take back some control over your thoughts, then you get a new perspective on how those thoughts make you feel. The more I still my mind in meditation and make it quieter, the more peace and the less stress I have.

For it to become a great tool for you, it will take concentration and practice – that is the hard part, but the benefits are worth it! You can meditate while sitting in a doctor's waiting room, at the airport waiting for your flight to some tropical island, or while waiting on your oil change. People will just think you are napping. Meditation can easily be worked into your daily life, and all it takes to get all the benefits is simple, daily practice.

There are some people who have tried meditation before and say that it does NOT work for them. Sometimes, they say it is too hard, or that they can never get their mind to settle down. So, IF you have tried meditation before and think it just doesn't work for you, then I may have the solution that helps you get back into a successful meditation practice.

Often, the mind is full of activity, ideas and images that are hard to control. That makes it hard for the body to settle down, too. Your mind and body *can* work together to enjoy the benefits of meditation, even if you have had trouble with meditation before. The solution is a type of meditation that I like to call "Moving Meditation." It is a meditation shortcut that will help you get instant benefits mentally without frustration. And from there, you can develop your meditation skills. I will explain more in just a bit.

But first, we will talk about exercise. Right now, you can put this book away and go take a 10-minute walk to make your life better. Seriously. If you do, just come back in a few minutes to find out why it works so well.

EXERCISE - When I was trying out new medicines for stress, depression, and anxiety, my doctor mentioned the benefits of exercise. I was a single mom with a disabled child. I did not want to go to a gym. I could not afford a gym anyway. As we continued the conversation, she told me something startling: for many people suffering from depression regular exercise can help just like medicine. That is an amazing statement!

(ATTENTION: If you take any sort of maintenance medicine please do not ever stop it without the direction and advice of your doctor. With many brain/psychological medicines, you must slowly taper down the dosage before stopping. You could trigger negative psychological, mental, or physical reactions because of abruptly stopping a medicine.)

When you take medicine for your brain you are attempting to alter your chemistry in a positive way. The hope is to make your stress, depression, anxiety, PTSD, or panic attacks more manageable and less severe.

We have all heard about the benefits of exercise. It decreases the risk of heart attacks and stroke. It can lower blood pressure, improve bone density, increase your metabolism, and help your joints stay flexible. Research is proving that it can reduce the risk of some cancers. It also is proving to reduce some problems associated with diabetes. There is even on-going research into exercise helping dementia patients curb the spread of their disease.

Exercise is good for your body. Well, your BRAIN is a part of your body! All the body benefits of exercise are not just for everything below the neck. Exercise alters your brain chemistry in a positive way!

Here is what my doctor told me:

- Exercise is effective and cheap!
- It can be an antidepressant in the short term AND long term.
- It is equally beneficial for both men and women.
- It is beneficial for all ages, but older people really get a great boost.
- Walking is just as beneficial as something more strenuous.

- It is most effective if you stick to it, so make it a part of your routine.

What if you hate the idea like I once did? Then start slowly. Set a reasonable goal – like exercise for 10 minutes several times a week. Get accustomed to a new routine and then move it up to 30 minutes.

There are many great types of exercise. You can try walking, running, or jogging. Or try yoga, a martial art, or I can teach you my personal exercise system! I even found that taking just a 10-minute stroll around the block made a difference. And when I could not go outside, dancing to the radio was the next best thing. The idea is to just get moving.

Taking a walk allowed me the chance to get my kid out on a bike. We created an exercise routine together. It was cheap and easy. I noticed an immediate positive effect. It made such a difference for me that I have included exercise in my weekly routine for the last 20 years. I exercise several times a week, but I balance it out with plenty of chocolate. Okay, I know that sounds like a joke, but it is true! I have always been a plus-sized woman, but that is another battle we can discuss in another book.

I dreaded getting up to go exercise, but I felt much better afterwards. I would remind myself how great I would feel when done. That kept me motivated. Now that I am older, I focus on stretching and low-impact exercise. Just start slow and build up to 30 minutes of exercise several times a week.

One note about starting an exercise program: check with your doctor first. Most doctors are going to be absolutely thrilled that you want to start exercising! But make sure they check you out before you start training for the triathlon.

I still do not go to a gym. I do chair yoga for chubby people. (I am writing a book on that.) I practice a strength and stamina-building routine that is based on Western mysticism. (That truly is a whole other book I just wrote.) I also have a treadmill in my bedroom, and I use a weighted hula-hoop, some hand weights and a twisty board. But taking a walk is still my favorite way to get moving. My exercise routine is easy and effective - just like the next beneficial tool.

<u>MEDITATION</u> - I truly credit meditation with saving my life. I began a daily meditation practice at a period of my life when I had little time or energy for doing something positive for myself. As a single mom with a disabled kid every moment focused on taking care of him. I barely had time for the necessities of life, much less something that I thought was a little weird. I had tried meditation years before, and remembered that it had helped when I was desperate and hurting after trauma. I am so glad that I took the chance to try again, because it saved my life and helped me save my son.

There are 7 meditations that I have used now for over 30 years. Each has helped me in tremendous ways.

1. The 10-minute "Power Nap"
2. A Walk on the Beach

3. Your Private Hideaway

4. Rainbow Sleep

5. 5x5x5

6. Be The Pebble

7. MM- Moving Meditation

Each are simple to use. All you need is a bit of practice. All have been invaluable in my healing process. The next three chapters have details about the first three meditations on the list. We will discuss "Rainbow Sleep" in the chapter on sleep issues. It is a quick visualization and relaxation technique that you use right before bed. It is easy enough that you can start using it tonight.

Meditations 5, 6 and 7, are QUICK and EASY enough to use right now. They are the fastest ways to meditate. I will teach them to you in this chapter, and you will be able to start getting the benefits of meditation immediately! You will find each of them so intuitively easy and helpful that you might wonder why you have never done this before. We will get to these in just a moment.

First, let's clear us a few misconceptions about meditation. Some people are afraid of meditation. They might be afraid of making changes or trying something that is different. Here in the West, some see meditation as a part of a non-Christian, religious experience.

Let me be very clear here - there is nothing in meditation or in anything we discuss in this book that goes against the teachings of the major religions and the spiritual masters. Meditation is about love, peace, reducing stress, becoming more fulfilled, and connecting with your inner, divine spirit. Those goals are in line with most religions!

I explained meditation this way to a very religious friend just a few days ago: *prayer is talking to God; meditation is listening to God.* In meditation, you learn to quiet your inner dialog, to still your mind. When your mind is racing, and you have a mile-long to-do list, then you do not have a chance to hear that still, small voice of inspiration. I hear that voice as a message from the Divine. You cannot hear the answer to any prayer if you are not listening. That explanation changed my friend's feelings about meditation.

When my young son was in the worst years of his immune disorder, during his first decade of life, I experienced some of the worst stress from active traumas and from past traumas. I was miserable, and I did not have time to be miserable. I also did not have time to sleep. The 10-minute deep meditation became my "Power Nap." It became a way for me to recharge and get ready for the next crisis. "A Walk on the Beach" and "Your Private Hideaway" also found their way into my bag of tools. Each is quite different, but both gave me new perspectives on how to help myself. In one of them you will meet a child. In the other you will drink deeply from a fountain.

MEDITATION INSTRUCTIONS - There are several types of meditations. You can meditate on your own without a guide or voice to give you instructions, but guided meditations are often easier for the beginner because someone else is helping you. That is often the best way to learn. We will discuss guided meditation in just a moment. First, we will take a look at my three quick and easy instant meditations that you can try right now.

These three simple exercises are an easy way for you to "sample" meditation and see what it is like. I call the first one "The 5x5x5" breathing exercise.

In just a moment, you will close your eyes and practice breathing in through the nose to the count of 5 seconds. You will then hold it for 5 seconds, and then release your breath through your mouth for 5 seconds. You can do this three times in a row, or ten times in a row. Do it until you feel a sense of calm.

I want you to focus on breathing deeply into your belly. Often, people take shallow breaths, just using the upper chest and shoulders. Instead, when you close your eyes for the 5x5x5 exercise, put your hands on your belly, and feel it expand with each breath.

That is how you will know you are practicing deep breathing. You may get a bit light-headed breathing this way, after all, you are bringing in a lot of oxygen and expelling a lot of carbon dioxide. It feels good, but don't jump up right after doing it. Are you ready to try it? Take a moment and see how it feels.

(Okay, how was it? Did you feel a sense of peace and calm? Did you notice that your shoulders relaxed and lost some of that tight feeling? Stop and try it again. See what other good feelings you feel!)

You can use the 5x5x5 technique when you are experiencing extra stress at work or at home. It takes only two or three minutes out of your day. The next exercise is also simple and takes only a few minutes of your time. It does not focus on your breath; it focuses instead on a simple visualization.

I call it: "BE THE PEBBLE!" In just a moment, you will close your eyes and start calmly breathing in through your nose and out through your mouth. As you just quietly and calmly breathe in and out, you will imagine a gently flowing stream. In that stream, there is a little pebble, right on the bottom. That little pebble is just spending time in the flow of the water. The pebble is not stressed out, it is not worried, it is not rushed. The pebble is just experiencing the water passing gently over and around it.

As you breath in and out, you will be the pebble. Just imagine you are the pebble and feel the warm and gentle water as it washes over you. That is all. Just enjoy that feeling of calm and peace until you are ready to open your eyes. Are you ready to try it? Take a moment and see how this one feels.

(Okay, how was it? Did you feel a sense of peace and calm? Could you imagine the gentle sunshine and the warm water? Stop and try it again. See what other good feelings you feel!)

Now you have experience with breathing techniques and visualization! Just these two simple exercises are enough for a lifetime of stress reduction. Use them often. Use them every day. I do. These exercises are my "go-to" stress busters when I have just a minute or two to spare. See how easy it is to take back some control over your stress levels and your thoughts!

If you had trouble with either of those meditations, then I have a third easy one for you to try. This is the "MM" Moving Meditation. If the problem with your meditation practice is that you cannot get your mind to settle down, then we will use this "hack" to make it easier! For so many people, they just feel jumpy or twitchy when they try to meditate. So, we will use that feeling instead of trying to ignore it. Let's MOVE in our meditation.

At first, this is best tried while sitting down. If you find that this type of meditation works for you, then you can actually use this technique while standing and even expand it into a walking meditation. (Just make sure and keep your eyes OPEN if you chose to do this as a walking meditation.)

Try this simple Moving Meditation right now. Sit in a comfortable chair, but scoot forward and sit at the front edge. Place your feet on the floor, a little wider than hip width. Make sure you are sitting firmly on the edge of the seat. Place your hands, palm down, on your knees. You can close your eyes or keep them open. Just breathe in through the nose, hold it, and then out through the mouth. This begins just like the 5X5X5 exercise.

The difference here is *movement!* With each in-breath, you will bring your arms up, with each out-breath, you will bring your arms down. If anyone was watching you – and no one is – it would look like a very slow version of "the wave" that crowds do at a packed concert or sporting event.

Now, instead of moving your arms up and down, you can try this another way. Open your arms up to the side with each in breath and then back to the center with each out breath. Imagine you are holding an inflating beach ball that expands and deflates with each breath. You can take this idea of meditation movement even further by swaying your torso back and forward along with your hands. Try it!

For some people, especially those who had have problems trying meditation before, this addition of movement can help manage the racing thoughts and the twitchy feelings that they get with traditional meditation. If this works for you, then use it! Because ANY meditation is better than no meditation.

To do this MM as a walking meditation, just find an unobstructed pathway in your home. Maybe you can walk a circle around your sofa or you have a long hallway that you can use. Walk slowly and steadily on your pathway. Coordinate your in and out breaths with your steps. I find that breathing in for three steps and breathing out for the next three steps is just right for me. Four steps might be better for you. If you have any sort of balance issues, then do not add the arm movements; just focus on taking steps and breathing. But if you can, add the arm movements, either up and down, or open outward and then back in.

When I have an especially difficult decision to make or I am just experiencing those restless anxious feelings that everyone feels from time to time, this type of moving meditation calms and recenters me. I kick off my shoes and socks, and for about ten minutes, I walk a pathway around my sofa and just breathe. Sometimes, my doggie Merlin even joins me.

(Okay, how was it? Did the racing thoughts and restless feelings go away? If you tried it only with the arm movements, try it again adding in the torso movements, and see if that helps, too. Find a pathway in your home and try it as a walking meditation, too.)

GUIDED MEDITATION INSTRUCTIONS - Of course, I recommend that you keep going with your meditation practice, because the three *guided meditations* and another visualization ahead can help bring even more transformation!

I would like to share with you a quick tutorial about guided meditation. You can read and practice these with a friend, a spouse, a partner, or even in a group. Once you get familiar with them you will be able to breathe deeply, relax, and be at peace anywhere. Practice and then you will be a master.

I recorded three guided meditations for you. Anyone can listen to them. They are free for everyone to use. Each meditation has a separate link, and it was produced with some gorgeous music from composer Kevin Macloud. If you are reading this book as an ebook, here is the direct link for the website - https://www.shannawarner.com/2020/08/13/1530/guided-meditations-that-i-love/. If you are reading this as a paperback or listening to the audiobook, then just go to whatever internet search engine you use and find ShannaWarner.com. Look for the blog post titled, "*Guided Meditations That I LOVE.*"

Another option is for you to record the guided meditations for yourself! Start by reading through the meditation. Then once you get comfortable with each script, you can record it easily on your computer or a rewritable CD. Once you have practiced the meditations several times, you will not need music or a voice to guide you at all. You can even write your own meditations and record them for your own personal use.

If you would like to make your own guided meditation, then start with a short script like the ones in the next chapters. If you do not like some of the wording or phrases, then feel free to change it up.

Practice reading it several times. Speak slowly and pause often. You may feel like it is too slow when you are reading it, but it will be exactly right when done.

Play some relaxing, instrumental music in the background. Do not play music with words. That will interfere with what you are reading. Do not play something energetic. This is not the time for the "William Tell Overture" or anything with a heavy, fast beat.

Practice reading the meditation with the music in the background. When you feel ready, make a recording. I made lots of meditation cassette tapes 30 years ago. Now you can easily record a file on most smart phones.

Another option is to record on your laptop or computer. There are probably speakers and a microphone built into the hardware. Many computers have a CD disc drive for using a rewritable CD. Do not be afraid to go ask for help. I bet you have a young person in your life who is tech savvy. Consult with them!

Once you are happy with the recording make sure and listen to it often, every day if you can. You will find that you can relax easier with more practice!

When you are ready to begin a mediation, I recommend that you lie down on your bed on your back. But you are welcome to sit in a comfortable chair. Whatever makes you the most comfortable is what is best. If you lie down, you just might fall asleep! You might want to set a timer for 15 minutes in case you do. Make sure to remove glasses, earrings, or anything that could slip off and be distracting. Close your eyes and breathe deeply for a few moments, in through the nose and then out through the mouth. When you feel relaxed, then you are ready to begin.

CHAPTER THEMES

Guided Meditation

Exercise

Be The Pebble

5X5X5

MM-Moving Meditation

.

CHAPTER 2:
WHY MEDITATION?

"Childhood innocence is shattered when you must take their hand and explain what death is, and how it might happen to them."

IN THE NEXT THREE CHAPTERS, I will be sharing with you my favorite meditations. Each one is good at helping you relax, and all are good at relieving stress. If you already know about meditation or aren't interested in learning, then just skip to chapter 6. But, if you haven't tried meditation, or you have tried and quit, I want to encourage you to take another look. Meditation saved my life. And it helped me save my child's life, too. Those are strong statements, so let me tell you a quick story about IGE disorders and stress.

By the time my infant was three months old, we knew something was very wrong. His pediatrician sent us to all sorts of specialists, from dermatologists to geneticists. They thought he might have a life-threatening genetic disorder. It was something else entirely.

Having a chronically sick child is incredibly stressful. It is a traumatic situation for the child and for the parents. We all have ways to cope, some good and some bad. I went into full "mommy mode" – learning everything I could about my child's disorders and how to help him. My husband returned to the coping mechanism he knew best: drugs. Before my son was two years old, his father and I divorced.

So, have you ever heard of anaphylactic shock or anaphylaxis? It is a life-threatening allergic reaction that kills people every year. We discovered that my son had an immune disease. He would have life-threatening allergic reactions to about ten different items, from foods to medicines to products. The first time it happened to my son I had no idea what was going on. But I knew he was dying right before my eyes. I was terrified that first time. (Actually, every time he has gone into anaphylaxis, I am terrified, but through the years he and I learned how to cope.)

That first time, we were having lunch at a restaurant where my husband was a manager. You know how babies like to have a little taste of what you are eating? Well, I gave my son a tiny taste of some whipped cream that was on a dessert. He was at that age where babies start trying solid foods like cooked carrots and peas. I did not think one tiny bite would be dangerous.

I was wrong. Within a few seconds he started making strange choking noises. There had been nothing solid in the whipped cream, I had made sure of that. There was a gurgling as his little throat was closing shut! He could not breathe. He was gagging and starting to turn blue.

The baby was still in his car seat, and I drove like a crazy woman with the emergency car lights flashing all the way to the doctor's office. The office was close by. That is why he did not die that day. They quickly gave my tiny infant a huge shot of epinephrine for a severe, life-threatening allergic reaction to dairy proteins. That is when our relationship began with the new specialist: our Immunologist.

The week before my first Mother's Day, we were in Dr. Jane's office. She was trying to get the baby's infections under control. She wanted him admitted to the hospital. His immune system was out of control. At times it was almost non-existent, letting strep and staph infections run rampant through his tiny body. At other times it was over-aggressive and caused anaphylactic shock. His immune system would react to common items as if they were diseases to fight against.

I spent my first Mother's Day in the hospital with my six-month-old infant. One evening, while I was alone and the baby was quietly sleeping amid the noise of the monitors, a hospital administrator came to see me. She had a very strange offer.

"I think it's time for our chaplain to come talk with you about what happens if your baby dies. Would that be okay?"

"Uh, NO! No, that is definitely not okay!" (I do not know any new mommy who would have been okay with that conversation. I certainly was not.)

I took a deep breath and spoke calmly, "I am not interested in hearing about my infant dying. That is not a conversation I want to have."

"Well, it could happen, and I just want you to be prepared."

"There is no way I can be prepared for my baby to die." She started to interrupt me, but I held up my hand. "Look, I know it is a possibility. I do understand that. But as long as I am alive, I will fight for my son to live, too."

"What will you do if he dies?"

"If he dies right now, I will stand up at his funeral and tell people I am the luckiest person there because

I got to know him and be his Mommy. That is all. That is all I can do."

She sent the chaplain in to talk with me anyway. The priest and I had a lovely conversation about life and death and the meaning of existence. We talked together for about an hour. All that time, while we were answering life's greatest questions, the baby slept in his sterile crib while life-saving medicines dripped into his body through the biggest vein they could find in his little bitty foot.

He survived that trip to the hospital and many, many others. I cannot even count how many Epi-pens, steroid pills and medicines we went through over the next fifteen years. We were caught in a literal life-and-death struggle. We were at the mercy of his immune system.

My son is now twenty-five! He lived, although he still has the same life-threatening medical disorder. He is happy, productive and no longer afraid of death. Neither am I. We faced it so many times together.

HOW did we become happy, productive and no longer afraid of death? Meditation. It made all the difference. It allowed me to relax, get a new perspective, recharge, calm my mind, and return to focus on my child. Now you know a small part of WHY meditation matters. Life is hard. You have stress at work and at home. When you add in the stress from traumatic episodes in life, like chronic illness, then that stress gets even worse.

When I came home from that first hospital stay, and I fully understood that my life, and my son's life would never be "normal," I began looking for ways to help us stay as happy and as balanced as possible. Meditation was MY salvation during that time. And I taught my son, too.

So, if you do not want to take the time to learn more about meditation right now, then please, at least know that you can come back to these chapters when you need them. Because trauma happens. Tragedy happens. Bad things can occur in one instant and your life will never be the same. And every person on the planet will have some tragedy in their life. The secret is to have the knowledge and the skills BEFORE the tragedy so that you can make it through with less stress and heartache.

CHAPTER THEMES:

Meditation

Chronic Illness

Anaphylaxis

Preparation for Tragedy

CHAPTER 3:
THE 10-MINUTE POWER NAP

"During meditation, your breath slows down and your whole body relaxes. You can find renewed energy after experiencing total relaxation."

THIS MEDITATION IS GREAT for deep relaxation during the day, so you might want to set a gentle alarm in case you fall asleep. This is more of a recharge, a reset when you are having a stressful day. It can be as restful as a nap for some people. For me, it was MORE restful than a nap because I did not feel groggy afterwards. Instead, I felt more capable and energized to deal with my son and his severe medical issues. Anytime he was able to take a nap, then I took this "Power Nap!"

If at night you routinely have trouble falling asleep you can do this meditation before going to bed. But please read the chapter on sleep issues first, because I think the sleep visualization in that chapter is better for bedtime.

Please remember that this meditation has been professionally recorded with music for you. Just go to my blog post on my website, and the links for all three of the guided meditations are available for you to use. And please feel free to share them with anyone else who might need them! This is a free resource for everyone.

https://www.shannawarner.com/2020/08/13/1530/guided-meditations-that-i-love

"The 10-Minute Power Nap"

Lie down on your bed.

Or sit in a chair if that is more comfortable.

Close your eyes.

Place your hands gently at your sides.

Lift your shoulders up tightly and then let go.

Let them relax.

Turn your head slowly from side to side.

Breathe in slowly through your nose.

Hold it for several seconds.

Then breathe out fully through your mouth.

Do that again.

Breathe in slowly through your nose.

Breathe in slowly and deeply.

And then breathe out through your mouth.

Continue to breathe this way throughout the meditation.

In through your nose.

And out through your mouth.

As you continue breathing this way,

You will notice that your muscles are beginning to soften and relax.

Tension is starting to gently fade away.

If you find that your mind wanders,

just bring your attention back gently to the sound of

my voice.

Now, I want you to imagine a warm gentle glow,

Beginning at the bottom of your feet.

Feel this warm glow spread across the bottom of your

feet.

Feel it spread across your toes and up into your

ankles.

Flex your feet and your ankles.

Now let go of that tension, let them relax.

Feel the tension leave your feet and ankles.

Let the warm glow continue up from your feet

And up onto your lower legs and knees.

Slightly tense your calf muscles and knees.

Now let go of that tension.

Let your legs fully relax.

Let that warm glow make them soft and heavy.

The warmth will continue spreading up your legs.

You will feel it spread up into your bottom and groin area.

Slightly tense your bottom and groin muscles, then let them go.

Let the muscles lose their tension,

As the warmth continues to spread.

Breathe in through your nose, slowly and deeply.

And breathe out through your mouth.

The lower part of your body is now heavy with relaxation.

The lower part of your body is covered with a warm, gentle glow.

Just like a soft blanket or like sunshine on a warm, spring day.

That gentle warmth now touches your fingers.

Slightly tense them, and then relax and let go.

They will feel heavy and relaxed at your side.

Enjoy the sensation as your hands and arms relax in the warmth.

The warm glow travels up to your elbows.

And it continues to spread up to your shoulders.

Slightly flex your shoulders,

And then let all that tension go.

Let your shoulders feel relaxed and soft in the warm glow.

Breathe in through your nose. Hold it.

Breathe out through your mouth.

The warmth at your shoulders will spread to your neck and jawline.

Feel all the muscles in your jaw soften and relax.

Feel the muscles around your eyes soften and relax.

Your head is covered with the warm, gentle glow.

Breathe in through your nose, slowly and deeply.

Breath out through your mouth.

Your entire body is now covered with the warm, gentle glow.

Let the gentle warmth cover you like a tender blanket.

Your body is now deeply relaxed.

Feel the peace as every part of your body, spirit, and mind is relaxed.

Breathe in through your nose, slowly and deeply.

And now, breathe out through your mouth.

You can stay in this moment of peace as long as you wish.

Take a few moments right now to enjoy the warmth and peace.

When you are ready, you will open your eyes.

When you are ready, take a moment to look around you.

Flex your hands, shoulders, ankles, and feet.

When you feel ready, get up and enjoy the rest of your day!

(End of Meditation)

I hope you enjoy that meditation as much as I do. It is now my favorite quick way to de-stress after a long day. Get ready now for the other two meditations. They are very different than this one. One is a therapeutic discovery meditation that is good to use when you need some hope and direction in your life. The other is a more detailed meditation for complete deep introspection, creativity, and relaxation.

CHAPTER THEMES:

Meditation

Deep Relaxation

Power Nap

Recharge

CHAPTER 4:
A WALK ON THE BEACH

"Meditation is a great tool to heal old emotional wounds. There is comfort in knowing that the past can remain the past, and it does not need to have power over your life in the present."

THIS THERAPEUTIC DISCOVERY TOOL is a variation of something I wrote many years ago, combined with imagery my doctor suggested, mixed with the views from my favorite beach walk on Grand Cayman back when I was in college. A Buddhist friend who had experienced childhood trauma suggested a meditation like this to me. When my therapist (and yes, I totally believe that therapy is a fabulous tool when needed) also suggested I try this type of meditation I decided that two recommendations in quick succession was a good reason to try. I am so glad I did. This has become one of my top tools when I want to completely de-stress.

The previous meditation was all about relaxation, but some meditations can be used for more than that. The goal of this guided meditation is self-healing and connectedness: mind-body, spirit-psyche, past-present. When those connections start happening, for some people it can be a little disorienting.

In the next few minutes, you are going to gain access to some of your deepest emotions. You might find you are emotionally sensitive when finished. This meditation, for me, is like listening to certain pieces of music or viewing certain pieces of art: the beauty can make you weep. Make sure you have time and space to reflect afterwards. Do not practice this meditation when you are under extra stress, very emotional, or have a heavy workload.

So, WHY even do it at all? That is a good question! It is SO worth it. It can help you understand who you are. It can help you understand what you need to work on. It can help you heal old wounds. This is my favorite healing meditation. You might choose to have a pen and paper close by, so you can write down the messages and ideas that are given to you.

This meditation is gender neutral. The recording I made is also gender neutral. If you choose to record it for your own use as a self-guided meditation, then substitute he/she, hers/his, etc, as desired to fit yourself and your group or audience.

Please remember that this meditation has been professionally recorded with music for you. Just go to my blog post on my website, and the links for all three of the guided meditations are available for you to use. And please feel free to share them with anyone else who might need them! They are free resources for everyone.

https://www.shannawarner.com/2020/08/13/1530/guided-meditations-that-i-love

"A Walk on The Beach"

Lie down on your back on your bed.

Or sit in a chair if that is more comfortable.

Close your eyes.

Place your hands gently at your sides.

Breathe in slowly through your nose.

Hold it for several seconds.

Then breathe out fully through your mouth.

Do that again.

Breathe in slowly and deeply through your nose.

And then breathe out through your mouth.

Continue to breathe this way throughout the meditation.

Imagine you are standing on a quiet, deserted beach.

You are totally at peace.

There is no stress. There are no problems.

There is just the warm sand between your toes,

And the sound of the waves.

As you walk along the beach,

the sun is just starting to go down.

Watch as the colors in the sky start to change.

From red, to orange and yellow,

Then into blue, and finally deep purple.

You look down at your feet and see a seashell.

Pick it up. What does it look like?

Notice the shape and the colors.

Now put it in your pocket and continue walking.

As you start walking again,

The waves gently roll in.

They gently slide out into the darkening ocean.

Breathe the air in slowly and deeply through your
nose.

Hold it, and then breathe out through your mouth.

You continue walking along the shore.

The waves continue lapping at your feet.

You are totally at peace and relaxed.

You look up into the sky as the first stars begin to twinkle.

Breath in through your nose, slowly and deeply.

Breath out through your mouth.

As you look down the shore,

You see a small figure walking towards you.

As they get closer, you notice it is the figure of a child.

The child stops periodically to pick something up.

The child is alone and yet seems perfectly calm and at peace.

You walk towards each other.

As you get closer, the child comes to stand directly in front of you.

The child slips their tiny hand into yours.

As you look down into their eyes, you know you are seeing yourself.

You were that child so many years ago.

The child smiles and sits down on the sand.

And empties out the pail of seashells.

You sit down too.

The child shows you the seashells it has been
collecting.

You remember the shell that is in your pocket.

You offer the shell to the child.

You get a smile of delight in return.

The child climbs into your lap and whispers in your
ear.

Listen intently to that little voice.

You will remember exactly what is said to you.

And then you whisper back.

The child looks up into your face, nods, and smiles.

Then stands up and starts gathering up all the
seashells.

The new one is placed on the very tip top.

You reach out to hug the child and say

That you will be back again soon.

The child waves goodbye and begins humming a song.

Skipping back down the shoreline,

The child turns one last time to wave to you.

You watch as the small figure quickly fades,

Into the shadows of the falling darkness.

You are still sitting on the sand.

When you look up again at the dark night sky,

There are millions of stars.

You lean back into the soft sand and close your eyes.

Now, breathe in through your nose, slowly and deeply.

Hold it, and then out fully through your mouth.

Breathe in again, slowly and deeply.

And then out through your mouth.

Enjoy this singular moment of clarity and peace.

You can stay on the beach as long as you want.

Take a few moments to enjoy the peace and quiet

When you are ready, you will open your eyes.

You will be back in your physical surroundings.

Take a few moments before you get up,

To stretch your legs and arms.

Now you are ready to get up.

Now you can continue with your day.

(End of Meditation)

I hope you have that notebook nearby. Go write down what the child said to you and how you responded. Whatever the child said to you was important. This is for your eyes only and no one else will know.

I learned quite a bit from my inner child's voice. The very first time I met her in this meditation, she comforted me and told me it was going to be okay when I grow up. It was a powerful meditation all those years ago and is just as powerful now. Try it. But you might need to have a tissue handy.

CHAPTER THEMES:

Meditation

Reparenting Yourself

Childhood Issues

Past/Present

CHAPTER 5: YOUR PRIVATE HIDEAWAY

"Meditation is like waking up from the best sleep you have ever had; it is like the smell of fresh air after a rainfall; it is like holding hands with someone who loves you."

THIS MEDITATION WILL TAKE YOU to a secret happy place inside your mind. You can visit there whenever you want. While the last meditation came with a word of caution, feel free to just jump right IN to this one!

This is a deep meditation, too, but the path to connectedness is different. Let me explain: the last meditation took you into your past and brought messages from your inner child. It was a deep dive into your interior memories and pain. This meditation is more about connecting with nature and creative forces in your mind that can bring healing and energy.

I LOVE this meditation. Usually, I change it up on a whim each time. You will see just how easy that is to do! The coolest thing about this mediation is that if you use this tool consistently, then objects will sometimes appear in your private space from one meditation to the next. It is always fun for me to go see what might have appeared since the last time. Each time I open the door, I know something wonderful will happen. This meditation can make you laugh, relax, and just have fun. Oh, and *always* drink deeply from the fountain.

Please remember that this meditation has been professionally recorded with music for you. Just go to my blog post on my website, and the links for all three of the guided meditations are available for you to use. And please feel free to share them with anyone else who might need them! They are free resources for everyone.

https://www.shannawarner.com/2020/08/13/1530/guided-meditations-that-i-love

"Your Private Hideaway"

Lie down on your back on your bed.

Or sit in a chair if that is more comfortable.

Close your eyes.

Place your hands gently at your sides.

Breathe in slowly through your nose.

Hold it for several seconds.

Then breathe out fully through your mouth.

Breathe in through your nose, slowly and deeply.

And then breathe out through your mouth.

Continue to breathe this way throughout the meditation.

Imagine you are standing at the start of a hidden, forest pathway.

The trees and bushes have grown together.

They have created a tunnel that is just your size.

The tunnel curves slightly to the left.

The dappled sun filters through the trees and bushes.

The pathway looks inviting, and so you go!

Walk down the pathway and through the tunnel.

As you walk, notice how the light sparkles.

Notice the songs of the birds.

Notice how the fallen leaves crunch beneath your feet.

As you come to the end of the tunnel,

You are now standing at the top of a rocky staircase.

You cannot quite see the bottom landing.

There is fog and mist at the bottom.

And there is a door.

You decide to take the first step.

Step 10.

Then you take the next few steps.

….9, …8,

With each step, you feel the solid structure beneath your feet.

…7, …6,

With each step you become more relaxed.

…5, …4,

Now, you can see the bottom step as the mist swirls at your feet.

…3, …2, …1.

You are at the bottom landing.

The door in front of you is locked.

What does it look like?

Make it any shape or size, color, or texture.

It is the door to your private hideaway.

Do you feel the key in your pocket?

It fits the door.

No one else can reach this door, and no one else has a key.

When you open it, you will be standing in your private, safe place.

Put the key in the lock.

And now, open the door.

What do you see when you open the door?

Make the scene anything you choose.

You are the creator.

Everything here will be exactly the way you want it.

This is your private, safe place.

Step inside and look around.

Shut the door behind you.

There will be one thing already here in your private space.

Listen. Can you hear the splashing water?

Do you hear the fountain?

There is a fountain splashing into a small pond.

It has clear, sparkling water, freely flowing right into the pond.

Walk to the fountain.

If you are thirsty then take a drink.

If you need a goblet then one will appear in your hand.

If you prefer to drink from your hands then do so.

It you want to plunge your face in the water then so be it.

Drink deeply from the fountain.

The water will satisfy you like no other drink.

As you drink, feel the water going down your throat.

Know that each drink gives you strength, protection, and guidance.

Drink deeply.

If you choose you can wade out into the pool.

It is shallow and warm.

You can enjoy the feeling of your feet in the water.

You can lie back and float away if you want.

You can come back any time

and float in your little private pond.

This is your private hideaway.

It is totally for you and you alone.

Look around. See all the wonderful areas you need to explore?

When you visit here you will make it exactly as you wish.

But for now, it is time to return to the door.

As you walk to the door remember the key is in your pocket.

When you get to the door, turn around.

Look back at your private space.

Now walk through the door and lock it behind you.

Put the key back into your pocket.

Whenever you need the key, it will always appear in your pocket.

Begin climbing the stairs, counting each one along the way.

1, 2, 3, 4, 5, 6, 7, 8, 9, 10.

When you get to the top level take a moment for a deep breath.

Breathe in through your nose, slowly and deeply.

Hold it, and then breathe out completely through your mouth.

Now walk back down the forest pathway,

And through the tunnel of leaves.

Enjoy once again, the dappled sun coming through the tree tops.

Enjoy the sound of the birds and the crunch of the fallen leaves.

Breathe in through your nose, slowly and deeply.

Breathe out completely through your mouth.

You are now back in your physical space.

Breathe in and out several more times.

When you are ready you will open your eyes.

Stretch your arms and legs.

When you are ready you will get up and enjoy the rest of your day.

Your private hideaway is always just a few steps away.

(END of Meditation)

This private place is yours to visit anytime you choose. Go back and change it as often as you like. No one else can get in. You can do anything there that you want. Go skinny-dipping, go fishing, whatever! Nothing bad happens there because YOU are totally in charge. Always drink deeply from the fountain. Let the water relax your neck and throat and imagine you are drinking the elixir of life. You will feel refreshed every time!

CHAPTER THEMES:

Meditation

Deep Relaxation

Healing Water

Connecting With Nature

CHAPTER 6:
WHY DO YOU FEEL THE
WAY YOU DO?

"When you stop and stare directly at your fears, you take back some of your personal power. You can say, "I lived through this and I will survive the next ordeal, too."

(Trigger Alerts – we will be using some strong language and discussing difficult topics in this chapter, especially sexual abuse, violence, and assault.)

PLEASE REMEMBER THAT I always recommend you contact a therapist, psychologist, or psychiatrist if you are experiencing severe stress from depression, anxiety, suicidal thoughts, panic attacks or any other severe stress symptom we might discuss in this book.

No one needs to define stress for you. Every single person on the planet experiences the part of human life, the human condition, that causes stress. And it can affect everyone - child, adult, male or female.

Even good things can cause stress. Any woman who has given birth knows this. Bringing a child into the world can be the biggest blessing in your life, and the biggest headache at the same time. And just ask any bride and groom planning a wedding, and they will tell you about stress and their wedding blues.

Those are normal stresses brought about by normal parts of life. It is a part of the human condition that we all experience. But I am specifically interested in showing trauma survivors how and why the steps to stress reduction in this book can help.

Life is hard, and if you experience trauma of any sort, well, that just makes it harder. I know.

House fires, a tornado, crimes, serious health issues, car accidents, surviving war, sexual assault - all of these can cause physical and emotional trauma. Domestic violence, childhood abuse or neglect, and the death of a spouse or loved one can also cause trauma. There are so many types of trauma experiences, but all of them can cause tremendous stress, with emotional and psychological damage.

Even though we are not dealing with children and their issues in this book, there are some skills here that can be beneficial for children. I taught my son how to do the rainbow sleep visualization and how to combat his nightmares. And we used art therapy for talking about his stress. Please keep a close watch for stress and anxiety in your little one and be proactive! Get them to a professional.

I am concerned that we are going to find the rates of stress and anxiety disorders ramping up to very high levels within a decade or two. I am starting to see news stories about school children developing anxiety issues after practicing active shooter drills at their schools. Think about how frequently we hear of a school going on lock-down due to an active shooter threat. Thankfully, the threat is usually in the nearby community and not in the building itself. But it is not a drill. The schools are having children take cover and be on high alert.

Think of our parents and grandparents' generation who had to practice nuclear war drills during the first cold war era. That was an external fear, from an external foe, and it never came to pass. (Although it still could. We live in a violent world!)

The threat of gun violence for children at school is not an external fear from an external foe, it is an internalized fear from the very community in which the child lives. I believe that threat is causing serious anxiety for our kids and our teaching professionals. I believe we will see a tremendous growth of the reporting of stress disorders in the future because of this.

Please be on the alert for those childhood issues, and do not hesitate to talk to your child's teachers who can recommend a therapist at school or in the community. Children are amazing and very resilient. But they can still develop anxiety, fears and stress that can follow them into adulthood.

I speak more about adult issues because of my personal experiences. I have experienced lasting effects from family issues, serious health issues and car wrecks. But the longest-lasting trauma effects for me began while I was in college.

When I was in my senior year of college, I was sexually assaulted. It was a warm, autumn night, and the campus was nearly deserted. It was fall break. A "friend" who worked in the athletic department called me and asked if I would come talk to him. We had met previously at an off-campus religious organization. He wanted to talk about philosophy and religion.

But actually, he had planned a gang rape. There were not many people still on campus, and there is no telling how many other girls he tried to call before he found his victim. It was horrific. Assault always is. But I escaped before the other evil-doers had a chance to abuse me.

That one incident was made worse by the reactions I got from family and friends. I was rejected and victimized all over by people that "should" have supported and loved me. I do NOT blame them, not now.

People are not often equipped or ready to deal with the reality of trauma. We like to pretend that bad things cannot or will not happen to us or to someone we love. But bad things do happen every day to people you love. And some day, you will experience trauma of some sort. This is why you need to develop positive coping skills now! You may not have experienced sexual trauma like I have, but you can still benefit from the recommendations in this book.

The most common trauma for women is sexual assault or lasting effects from childhood sexual abuse. I have seen all sorts of statistics about the incidence of sexual assault in our country. Some say that one in three women will experience a sexual assault in their lifetime, and some think it is as high as 50%. I personally think it might be even higher than that!

Post-traumatic stress disorder (PTSD) can develop in people who have lived through stressful, traumatic experiences. Most people have a negative, stress reaction after a traumatic event. That is normal! But not everyone develops PTSD.

Most of the information we first knew about trauma and PTSD came from the studies of our Veterans as they returned home from war. Families spoke in hushed tones about how they had "shell-shock." It was a common term to indicate they had suffered some severe traumas and returned as changed men. These veterans had what now we would call PTSD. These types of stress reactions have contributed to an increasing rate of suicide among our veterans.

As researchers started to study the effects of sexual assault on women, they noticed something interesting: the reactions they saw in women were common to what combat veterans were experiencing. Different trauma situations created the same sort of negative reactions. Trauma experiences, whether they are experienced in childhood or adult life, can cause similar negative reactions.

Not every person reacts to stress from trauma in the same way. One person may be more likely to have nightmares and another more likely to become suicidal. It is different for each person because each brain is so different. There are some common symptoms, but not every survivor will experience every symptom.

After trauma, a survivor could feel shock, confusion, denial, anxiety, and numbness. Survivors might feel shame and guilt. Or anger, invasive thoughts, memories, and nightmares. You might have physical symptoms such as trembling, dizziness, sweating, or even a rapid heartbeat. There can be an awful combination of flashbacks during the day and nightmares at night. Add in hypervigilance, hyperarousal, and depression, and you can develop a devastating condition.

Feeling numb, sad, and angry are normal, understandable reactions to horrible things in your life! Those bad feelings may also mean that you cannot feel happy or excited at the things that once made you feel that way. Stress can take away your good feelings and give you awful ones.

Your mind might have a tough time processing what happened. It may bring up vivid memories of the event that feel real, like it is happening all over again. That memory can be triggered by anything that might remind you of the original trauma. Often, survivors will try to avoid people or situations that remind them of it. You might get to the point where you avoid places and situations just so you do not have to face that trigger. Avoidance can interfere with work, school, and relationships. Or you might just try to avoid thinking about the issues at all and become a workaholic or turn to drugs to numb your feelings.

When these issues disrupt your daily life and prevent you from getting help, then you might be developing a stress disorder like PTSD. It could also be symptoms of acute stress, generalized anxiety, depression, or panic disorder. I do not know how many different classifications of mental disorders there are. But I do know that every person will experience the after-effects of trauma differently. And it can disrupt your life for a long time. There is a great government website that has wonderful information about PTSD. There is more information in the Resources chapter at the end of the book.

It is normal to feel awful when awful things happen. But how do you know if you have an anxiety disorder or PTSD? Your reaction might be more severe and last longer. How long ago was the original trauma? I know other survivors of sexual abuse who still have flashbacks and nightmares 30 years after the event. So, if the reactions from the original trauma have stuck around, then get help.

Now you know why you, or your loved one, feels the way they do. Stress is a common part of life. But it can become overwhelming. The stress that comes from trauma can cause all sorts of awful feelings. You are taking steps right now to make your life better. That willingness to be pro-active can make a positive difference in your life. As you develop positive coping skills and become stronger, you will become better able to handle the normal stresses and additional traumas of life. And the beautiful part is that as you grow stronger, you will be able to help those around you. I am proud of you for even thinking about making your life better! You are stronger than you even know.

CHAPTER THEMES:

Sexual Assault

PTSD

Depression

Trauma

Strength

CHAPTER 7:
A MEMORY BOX IN A
MEMORY PALACE

"Your experiences, both negative and positive,
have shaped who you are. Let's un-cover, un-learn
and re-shape the bad parts of life!"

JUST TALKING ABOUT DIFFICULT issues can
cause stress for some people, it can bring up some
negative feelings. If you routinely talk about your
traumas, then your brain might "feel" the trauma as if
it was happening again. Think about a time you told a
friend or your spouse about someone at work that was

mean to you. Just telling the story again made you mad! Well, thinking about and talking about trauma can sometimes make you feel the pain all over again.

If you keep all your feelings bottled up, then they become buried in your heart and spirit, and that limits healing. There is a fine line inside your own brain when you talk about negative subjects. Talking about bad stuff, getting it all out in the open is often a good way to heal, but if the constant recitation of pain, the constant talking about bad stuff and issues makes you feel like it is all happening again, well, who wants to do that? And the answer is – no one.

It is important to deal with issues, especially stress and trauma, so you can make it better. And it takes courage! Whether you go see a therapist, a pastoral counselor, a psychiatrist, your family physician, or you read self-help books like this one, what you are doing is courageous.

It does not bother me one bit to talk about difficult issues. Not anymore. So how can I talk about all my stress-producing experiences, like molestation, rape and assault without the emotional feelings kicking in? How can I do this now without experiencing all the stress that goes along with those subjects?

You already know that exercise and meditation are part of the answer. Another part is the funny little habit of making a memory box to place in a memory palace.

What is that? It is a place in your mind where you can store ideas, thoughts, images and experiences. It is an ancient memory device, developed thousands of years ago. I first read about it when I was in high school. I needed something to help me memorize scripts and speeches. (It's one of the ways I memorize poetry. If you ever come to one of my seminars, I recite poetry for the audience.)

You basically create rooms with trails and routes between them in your memory. You can imagine your actual house, or a house you grew up in, or an imaginary location to base your memory palace on. On any route or trail, you can have as many rooms as you want. And in the rooms, you can have shelves. On those shelves, you can have boxes. You just store your memories wherever you want in your memory palace.

So, I have a dusty room in my palace where I keep some old memories that once were painful. I keep those memories in a box in my mind. I can take them out and look at them if I want or need to. And I can put them back into the box. There is molestation in there, and the gang rape I escaped from, and there is another sexual assault at a sister's house. There are some other difficult things in there, too, like some gun violence, my child's life-threatening illness and the death of my last husband.

It is just a way to take back some control over the things that hurt me. I can uncover and look at any painful issue when or if I need to, and I can put them back in the box when I am done. I do not ignore the issues, I manage them. My goal is to learn from the bad, UN-learn the parts that have hurt me the most, and then reshape my future as I move on from the past!

I want to take the bad in my life and re-shape it to something good. If it is impossible to make it good, then at least I want to make it beneficial for me. This is the ultimate trick of making lemonade out of lemons! Have you ever heard that little saying? How true it is. Our goal is to take the awful things that life has given us, and make it better - lemonade out of lemons. Not every tool or technique I mention in this book will help every person. Every brain is different, and what works for me (like the memory palace) might not work for you. But you will never know if you do not try!

You know that I consider exercise one of the best treatments for my mental health. But sometimes people get so depressed that exercise might seem impossible. That is when medicine might make a bigger impact for someone.

Depression is more than just feeling "sad." I remember a family member telling me that I needed to "snap out of it." (If it was that simple, then no one would ever be depressed. No one would need this or any other book.) Stress in life can lead directly to depression. Many people experience overwhelming feelings of worthlessness, hopelessness, or they even have thoughts of suicide.

Trauma survivors might also have a panic attack. That is an overwhelming feeling of fear that can strike without any warning. In the next chapter, we will discuss three techniques for battling panic attacks. But remember that those techniques are good for dealing with more than just panic attacks. I use them for battling depression and general anxiety issues also.

CHAPTER THEMES:

Memory Palace

Memory Box

Lemonade from Lemons

Taking Back Control

CHAPTER 8:
BATTLE THE PANIC

"You have no power over the random activities of life. Sometimes, bad things happen. You DO have power over your own attitude, your own motivation, and your own choices."

PANIC ATTACKS? THAT WAS a big issue for me! I would have physical symptoms like dizziness, trembling, and a rapid heartbeat. Usually a panic attack would happen when I was out with my son. I was hypervigilant about his medical issues. He nearly died so many times and it seemed like I was always in a "fight or flight" mode. That is where the body is full of adrenaline and is getting prepared to either battle the enemy or just run away. My anxiety about my son spilled over into panic attacks for me.

I even had panic attacks in my sleep! Nightmares AND panic attacks while I am supposed to be sleeping? Great. The only good thing about panic attacks is that they do not usually last long. Even though it feels like an eternity while they are happening, they typically only last a few minutes. I do not think the body can handle that full-on adrenaline preparedness in the "fight or flight" scenario for long.

A panic attack is scary. Some people with untreated panic disorders spend their lives inside. The fear of having an attack is so overwhelming that they will not leave their home. That is an extreme phobia level. Even if you are not at the extreme level it can still diminish the quality of your life.

What makes panic attacks even worse is that you can have a panic attack about the possibility of having a panic attack! How awful is that? It is like a self-fulfilling prophecy or a never-ending loop of anxiety. Well it needs to end!

Dr. Aaron Beck developed a tool that can help you be more A-W-A-R-E when dealing with anxiety and panic attacks. (More information about this technique is available in the Resources section at the back of the book.) Once you have learned this tip about being more aware, then I will share with you the 3 practical techniques I use to put that into action.

AWARE is an acronym that stands for: Acknowledge, Watch, Act, Repeat, Expect. First, you must Acknowledge your anxiety. Quit fighting it. Accept it as an emotion that everyone experiences in life. I learned that telling myself, "don't freak out," usually made me freak out more. (How ironic, I know.) I learned instead to give myself permission to have anxiety. I would tell myself instead, "Okay, I am feeling really scared right now. I know my nervous system is working overtime right now. I will be okay."

The next part is WATCH. Try not to judge your anxiety as good or bad. Instead, step back and watch it a minute and try to give it a rating. Use a scale of 1-100, and you will start noticing that all your anxiety is not the same. You will start to see patterns, and you will start to see when it decreases. You will be able to see what triggers your anxiety and what helps make it better.

Next in the acronym is ACT. Do not let your anxiety prevent you from living your life. Trying to always avoid anxiety can make it worse. If you try to avoid situations that make you anxious then you never learn how to tolerate the uncomfortable feelings and get past them. It feels good to avoid a bad situation or a bad feeling, but you might actually get caught in a loop of avoidance that reinforces the anxiety reaction. So, go out there and live your life with confidence and courage!

Next are REPEAT and EXPECT the best. Just do it again. It takes a lot of practice to learn to accept and deal with your anxiety. I know. I have been practicing for decades. And it does get better! Part of getting better is the expectation that it will. Each time you battle the panic and win, celebrate that win. Notice even the little things that get better, and eventually, the little things will build up into something big. Each episode is a fresh chance to practice being aware and in charge!

Along with that awareness, there were three things that worked for me in combatting my panic attacks. Please remember that many of the stress and trauma disorders have some symptoms in common. These three techniques are not just for anxiety and panic attacks. Each beneficial skill you learn could help in more than one area of your life! The first three are techniques I developed along the way for dealing with the panic attacks. My doctor helped me with the fourth technique. It is a thought process that I still use today in battling general anxiety. We will discuss the first three now, saving the last one for the chapter on sleep issues.

The four techniques are:

1. Break It Down
2. Breathe It Out

3. Imagine Deliciousness

4. Logical Conclusions

The first three techniques are three steps that I would combine into my panic attack management system when I was out in public. When I would feel those tingly, jangly, panic attack feelings start, I would "Break It Down." This meant that I would take the situation and turn the desired endpoint into tiny, manageable steps.

Here is an actual example from my life. I was out with my young son at a park. We were getting ready to leave. A man walked by who reminded me of a rapist from long ago. He was just enjoying the park with his dog. But I felt the panic rising. I became very AWARE of the panic and started watching my reaction. I also started a mental checklist of what I needed to do to get to the car. The car was my safety point. It was where I needed to go to feel better.

Checklist: I needed to gather up my stuff. I needed to pack up our snacks. I needed my kiddo to get his gear. I needed to get my keys out. I needed to walk calmly to the car. And presto, we were there; panic attack managed.

Breaking it down into little steps allowed my brain to focus on the checklist. It helped to calm the rising panic. It helped me to step back and watch the anxiety as it was building and as it was diminishing. Even though I was feeling fully anxious, I was acting in a positive manner to help myself. At the same time, I was adding the next tool which is "Breathe It Out."

When you start to physically tense up with a panic attack or with general anxiety you might have some trouble breathing. When you do not have enough airflow in your lungs because of tension, then all your body suffers. This includes your brain. Managing your breathing in an anxiety situation is particularly important. It is one of the best tools for managing panic, stress, depression, and all sorts of negative mental attitudes and issues. Remember the 5X5X5 technique for breathing? This is very similar, just used in a different way and in a different situation.

When the panic would start, I would tell myself that I am going to breathe OUT the panic and breathe IN the peace. With each breath in, I would mentally say, "PEACE." That was the best calming word for me. Maybe your calming word in this situation is different, and that is okay! Maybe your calming word is a name, perhaps the name of your deity, or maybe your calming word is "CALM." Whatever works for you is exactly what you need to use. Experiment and see what helps.

Then finally, Imagine Deliciousness is a way to visualize a positive image in your mind and help decrease the panic. As you are working on the first two steps, breaking down your actions into steps and focusing on breathing out the bad feelings, you add in a positive mental image.

You can create a happy picture in your mind! In the earlier chapter on meditation, we talked about visualization. You practiced being a pebble in a little happy stream, and letting the water flow over you. You can use that exact imagery to foster a sense of calm and manage the rising panic. Each time you breath OUT the panic, as you are breathing IN the peace and calm, you add a positive mental image.

I must confess to you that the happy picture I would usually visualize was food. I really hate to admit that, but it is true. And yes, you might guess that it was usually something chocolate!

I would visualize a slice of this wonderful chocolate cake that I make. (And yes, I would be happy to share the recipe with you! Just ask.) I would breathe in and imagine I was smelling that cake. I would work on my checklist and fight the rising panic. Breathing slowly in and out, using my calming word, and thinking of that wonderful smell, helped to calm my mind and get more oxygen into my body. Just having more oxygen helped to calm the rising panic.

Now, instead of chocolate cake, I have learned to use the scent of essential oils to help calm my anxiety. (Although my chocolate cake is truly fabulous!) Certain scents might help you, too. Maybe orange or lavender is a calming scent for you. You can purchase a little necklace where you put one drop of essential oil on a felt pad and it lasts throughout the day. My son got one of those for me, and I love it. Even when I do not have it on, I find that just thinking of a special scent helps to calm me down. It is an amazing aspect of our fabulous brains that we can just imagine a smell and it can help. Amazing. The power of the imagination is incredible.

There is also a great calming technique that uses touch. Sometimes, you can use an object like a bracelet, a ring or a lucky penny in your pocket to help give you a sense of calm. Have you seen someone wearing a rubber band on their wrist? That can be used to "snap" you back into a calmer state of mind. As long as you just snap it gently, then it can help you refocus away from the anxiety and towards more peace and calm. A spinner ring or a bracelet with some helpful words can be used to help manage your anxiety also. Just make sure to have several tools that work for you. (Just in case you forget one day to carry your only lucky penny or wear your only bracelet or essential oil necklace.)

Becoming more aware, and those three techniques worked wonders for me when I was out in public. The third helped more when I had panic attacks at night that woke me from my sleep. It is possible that the night-time panic attacks I experienced were a result of nightmares. I would wake from a deep sleep without any memory of a nightmare, so they seemed like separate issues for me. I battled those panic attacks and won! We will discuss that last technique – Logical Conclusions – in Chapter 10.

CHAPTER THEMES:

A.W.A.R.E. Method

Break it Down

Breathe it Out

Imagine Deliciousness

Essential Oil Usage

CHAPTER 9: UNEXPECTED TRANSFORMATION

"Tragedy, trauma, loss, and death, can teach us to appreciate life and love even more."

I NEEDED ALL THE GOOD SKILLS I had developed to deal with panic attacks because of a period of stress that I was unprepared for. That is how it happens, though. We are not always prepared for some of the tragedies of life. The panic attacks and nightmares tried to come back during a severe period of stress that was unexpected.

After my son was grown, educated and launched into his new life, I got remarried. I had been a single mom for sixteen years. My husband, David, and I were married only 11 months when he passed away unexpectedly. It was a shock. He died on a Saturday morning, and that Friday we had just made a five-year plan for careers, our relationship and retirement.

David had been a trauma survivor, too. When he was a young man, he had been involved in a train wreck. His body was full of pins and bolts holding his bones together. He lived with a lot of pain. We both used meditation and exercise to manage our stress. He was always in pain due to the physical scars and damage from the wreck. He also had emotional pain from child abuse and bad choices he had made in his young adult life.

He slept alone in bed the night he died. I offered to sleep on the sofa so he could really stretch out and get comfortable. When I got up that morning he was not breathing. His fingers and lips were blue. I could not rouse him. I could not move him. He was gone.

How can you see someone one night in the prime of their life, and then the next morning everything changes? It was surreal. That is the nature of death. It can come for each of us in the blink of an eye. I had faced the possibility of my son's death many times. I had saved his life many more times that I can count on my fingers. My husband's death was a new concept for me to adjust to. It was terrifying. I was devastated. My biggest supporter and cheerleader was now gone.

I called 911 and all sorts of emergency vehicles showed up: police, fire, and ambulance. The medical responders ran in to the bedroom. It was total confusion. They pumped him full of all sorts of medicines. They worked on him for about 45 minutes with a whole team switching out for chest compressions.

A physician was ready by phone to pronounce his time of death. But at the last moment one medic said,

"I heard a heartbeat." One heartbeat was enough for them to whisk him off to the hospital. I do not know how long he had been without oxygen before I found him, but I believe they took a dead man to the hospital.

I headed to the hospital right behind the ambulance. My son picked up his girlfriend, and they met me there. The three of us stood vigil in a cold, waiting room while a hospital emergency team tried every possible life-saving procedure. Finally, after about an hour, the emergency room physician came in to talk to us. David was brain dead. There was absolutely no activity. His body had been pumped full of drugs and a ventilator was pumping him full of air. But none of it could bring him back.

David did not have any written directions about what to do in a medical emergency like this. The doctor asked us if we knew. We all knew that he did not want to be hooked up to machines. That was one of the deepest fears he had expressed to us. The emergency department doctor made the decision to

NOT admit him to the regular hospital. Instead they would honor his wishes and remove him from all life-support.

The doctor asked me if I was strong enough to go back and see him one last time? Was I strong enough to be there when they officially pronounced him dead? I told him I was. Usually, emergency rooms are full of the hustle and bustle of nurses and doctors scurrying around saving lives. This one was surreally quiet, except for the beeps of machines and the flashes of light.

The nurse warned me it would probably take less than a minute for his body to completely shut down after the removal of life-support. It was true. It was over in less than a minute. I stood by his side and told him to get some rest, leave all the pain behind, and tell his Grandma that I loved my ring.

So, remember when I told you that good things can still happen in the bad times? Beauty can happen after tragedy. The most magical thing happened in the hour after his death! I am still amazed when I think of what I saw. His body was brought to a private viewing area next to our family waiting room. Over the next hour while we waited for family to get to the hospital there was an amazing transformation.

For the last twenty-six years of his life, he had been in near-constant physical and emotional pain. My brother and I watched as every line in his face relaxed. His face became one of total and absolute peace. The little pain lines disappeared from around his mouth and his eyes. You could see the handsome man as he really was, totally at peace.

It was a transformational moment for me. Yes, I understand the physiology of the death of the body, but it seemed that there was something happening. It was a last little message from him, a message that his death brought total peace and cessation of all pain. My brother and I stood at his side and watched as he became a young handsome man without a care in the world. He became his essence. His true nature was there for us to see. And it was beautiful.

There were waves of grief in the weeks after his death. There have been books written about stages of grief, but for me, grief was more like waves. At first, it was like a tsunami, a violent wave that destroys all life and carries away all happiness. Throughout the day, there might be smaller waves, less destructive waves, as a certain memory would flow over me. Eventually, the waves settled down and became more like the gentle tickle of the warm sea water on the beach. The waves come in and they go out. That is how my memories of him are now.

But in the tsunami waves immediately after he died, there was one specific moment where I nearly had another panic attack. At some point I knew I had to clean up his car. It was a red, sporty car that he loved. You know how when someone has a personal possession then somehow their scent lingers? Well, the car smelled like him. I had no idea how much it would affect me.

When I opened the door of his car, the very scent of him caused me to weep. And then flashes of memories came. Then came the pain, such tremendous pain. And then anger! I turned on the car and turned up the radio. Then I screamed until I was hoarse and could not scream anymore. I decided to leave the cleaning for another day. Instead I went inside and wrote him a letter. Yes, I know that writing to a dead man sounds weird. But you know what? It was the most beneficial tool I had during that mourning process. (And just get ready, because later in this book, we will be doing some beneficial writing together!)

I was already accustomed to the idea of death because of dealing with my son's medical disorder. I was accustomed to the idea of emotional pain. I did not run away from uncomfortable feelings. I dealt with them. I looked at them. I said hello to them. I said hello to quite a bit of anger! I was mad as hell. Every time I felt a seething anger rising inside, I would ask myself, "Why? Why am I mad as hell today?"

It was easy to answer that question. I was mad because I was abandoned by death, because we had just made plans, because he was only 46, because he was my number one cheerleader, because he believed I could do anything. Every time I felt that anger, I wrote a letter to him. Can you guess how many letters I wrote? I wrote a letter every day for 100 days. (And someday I will write a book about it. I will share that process of grief with you.)

During that letter-writing process I went from anger to acceptance. And I went from acceptance to gratitude. I became grateful that I had met him and that we had been able to be together in that brief little bit of time.

I never hid from my feelings or pretended they did not exist. I was aware of every feeling. I watched every feeling. I rated it. How am I feeling today? How was I feeling yesterday? I let every feeling speak to me. During the process of writing just one letter I might feel denial, anger, bargaining, depression and acceptance! And once each feeling had spoken to me, once it had given me a message, I let it go. And then I healed.

It was during this time of stress when nightmares tried to come back into my life. I was battling grief, along with depression and anxiety during the day. It took every bit of my skills - the meditation, exercise, refocusing on positive words and phrases, breaking it down, breathing techniques – it took all those skills to keep the panic at bay during the day. But at night? Your conscious brain is asleep, and your subconscious is in charge.

Difficulty with sleep has always been a sign that my anxiety is getting worse. It was also a trigger for making the depression worse. When you cannot sleep, then you cannot rest. When you cannot rest, then your mind and body cannot repair itself.

Managing my sleep issues became vital to my mental and physical health. In the next section we will talk about the third technique I mentioned at the beginning of this chapter, Logical Conclusions, along with other tips for quality sleep.

CHAPTER THEMES:

Death of a Spouse

Wave theory of Grief

Transformation

Journaling/Writing

CHAPTER 10:
BETTER SLEEP TONIGHT

"A great night's sleep is elusive for many people. How many grumpy attitudes or accidents could be prevented by a few good zzzzzs?"

AS AN ADULT I DEVELOPED an anxiety disorder about the process of falling asleep. As a child I learned a common little prayer. You may have taught this same prayer to your children. Well, it terrified me as a child.

"Now I lay me down to sleep;

I pray the Lord my soul to keep;

If I should die before I wake;

I pray the Lord my soul to take."

Why did that prayer frighten me so much as a child? I think it was the part saying that death in my sleep was a possibility. What little child needs to hear that? Yikes. That prayer did not bring me comfort. As a child I got past the fear, but it returned in my adult years.

Part of my adult sleep issues stemmed from dealing with my son's medical disorder. At one point, when he was about two years old, he had an allergic reaction (Anaphylaxis or Anaphylactic Shock) to a new medicine in the middle of the night. I might have awakened to a dead child if I had not heard him struggling to breathe in the middle of the night. The necessary hyper-vigilance I had to maintain to keep him alive spilled over and caused a near-phobia about sleep for me as an adult.

I became so afraid of falling asleep that I developed severe insomnia. And no, I absolutely do NOT like prescription sleeping medicines! I have tried several. I do not like the way I feel the next day. There is only one sleep aid that I will use now. It is not a prescription. It is an all-natural sleep product that contains melatonin.

(If you want more information about it or any of the other non-prescription products I use, then send me a private message on Facebook or an email and I will get the information to you. My contact information is available in the Resources section at the end of the book.)

When I would wake up with a panic attack in my sleep or when I would have trouble falling asleep because of fear that I (or my son) would die, I would use that third tool I mentioned in the last chapter. I call that tool "Logical Conclusions."

This tool is a way to train your brain to not over-react to stress! This use of this tool might sound a little harsh at first. But let me explain it and tell you how I used it. This may NOT be something you ever want to try, but it works for me! (Please remember to consult first with a professional if you are experiencing any signs or symptoms of panic disorder or night-time panic attacks.)

When I was afraid of something specific, like the imagery from a nightmare, I would imagine what would happen if that thing truly came to pass. I would take the subject of my worry and think about it all the way to the endpoint - to the logical conclusion of that situation. I would do this during the day when I was fully awake. I would do this during the day when I was in a happy place and not having any extra stress. I would do this as a part of the management of my memory palace.

Do you remember when we talked about memory palaces? You can take some difficult ideas, images, worries, fears and experiences, and place them in a box on a shelf in a room in your memory. Then, you can take them out whenever you need or want and look at them. If you start to feel panic or anxiety, then you just put them right back in the box.

I would use that technique of putting my nightmares and night fears into a box. Instead of worrying about dying in my sleep, I would imagine what would happen if I DID die in my sleep. Instead of worrying about being in a plane crash, I would imagine what would happen if I was. This is uncomfortable to do at first, but a nightmare or a night panic attack is far more uncomfortable!

This was the tool I used when I woke up from a deep sleep in a full-blown panic attack. I do not think there was anything more frightening for me than those panic attacks in my sleep! When you wake up with a nightmare you know why you are awake. You can think through the nightmare and eventually get back to sleep. (We will discuss combatting nightmares in just a little bit.)

When you wake from a deep sleep in a full-blown panic attack it is totally disorienting. You have no idea if there is a reason for the panic or not. Maybe there really *is* an intruder. Maybe your house really *is* falling down. Maybe someone really *is* dying. It is truly an awful situation. But once you discover that all is well, then you still need to get back to sleep.

Logical conclusions allow you to imagine a scenario and then be okay with it. I know it sounds a harsh to say, okay, I can imagine I am dead or someone I love is dead and I am okay with that. But here is the secret: *after a while you help your brain to not over-react to the possibility of tragedy.* (Read that last sentence again. Remember, this is our goal – helping the brain to react less to stress and have more peace. We are uncovering and unlearning the negatives, and recreating more helpful ways to move into the future!) I can now consider the possibility of dying in my sleep. Or of being raped again. Or of the unexpected death of someone I love. And I can do this without overwhelming anxiety or panic.

I can imagine the logical conclusions of what I would or would not do, what would or would not happen. Being able to fully imagine any situation allows me to look at it, dissect it, and deal with it. I got to the point where if I woke up from having a panic attack, I could easily get back to sleep. I would tell myself, *"Well, if I die in my sleep, then I will be free of ever having another damn, freaking panic attack in my sleep!"* And that little bit of logic really helped me cope.

Eventually I got to the point where I could say, *"So what! I do not even care. I cannot control every situation that will or will not happen! I cannot live my life afraid of the possibilities."* There is a little slice of freedom in those statements! There is so much in life that you and I cannot control. Why would I want to spend my precious time worrying about all the things I genuinely cannot control? Why would you?

This technique became vital to me in the weeks after my husband died. I had battled and won against panic attacks in the day and in the night. Then, when he died, that level of stress tried to bring anxiety, panic, and depression back into my life.

I began focusing more on how to sleep well. HOW to make my lonely bed a quiet place for rest and repair. Remember how the Logical Conclusions technique teaches us that we cannot control everything in life? Well, we cannot control everything in death, in our sleep, in our child's life. There is so much that we cannot control. Instead of that fear and that knowledge overwhelming you and causing you to just give up, let it instead help you refocus on the things that you CAN control.

What can you control? Your attitude. What you read. What you put into your mind and body. What thoughts you focus on. Exercise and meditation. All of those are things YOU CAN CONTROL. Here is another tip and technique for better sleep that you can control: *create your own bedtime routine.*

As parents we do this for our children. They get a nice warm bath and a snack. Then their teeth get brushed and it is time for a story. Now you get to do this for yourself. When you make a routine for your bedtime it helps your body and mind relax and get ready for rest. As you think about creating a bedtime routine here are a few things to remember:

- Limit the electronics. All that light is a distraction for your brain.

- End the late-night snacks. The food could cause indigestion anyway.

- Limit your liquid intake. It will just interrupt your sleep when you must get up to go pee.

- Think about *not* watching the local nightly news. I do not! It is filled with stories about crime and scary statistics.

- Do not read in bed. An exciting novel will just keep you awake.

- Keep the bedroom for sleep and sex. (Keep if comfortable and sensual.)

- If you must get up in the night keep the lights low.

- If you cannot quickly get back to sleep, get out of bed and try reading a boring book for a few minutes. That might do the trick.

- Play some calming music.

- Think about getting a sound machine to generate white noise.
- Try to keep to the same times for going to bed and getting up each day to help set up the routine.

In the section on Meditation, I mentioned an easy visualization technique that I use to help me get to sleep. My "Rainbow Sleep" visualization is so easy to do that you can use it tonight! ROY-G-BIV: red, orange, yellow, green, blue, indigo, and violet. Those are the colors of the rainbow.

If you can visualize the colors in your mind, then this will be quite easy for you. If you cannot easily visualize them then I will give you a memory trick that will help make it easier - especially if you have a bowl of fruit. Yes, fruit.

The goal of this visualization is to imagine yourself floating through each color of the rainbow and then floating off to sleep on a cloud. You imagine yourself as being light and fluffy as you float off to sleep. The colors of the rainbow also coincide with the body's energy centers that are often a focus of meditation. By the time you visualize all the colors and see yourself floating away on a cloud, you will have calmed every energy center in your body. Your body and mind will both be relaxed and ready for sleep.

"Rainbow Sleep" Visualization - As you lie in bed each night practice seeing the colors of the rainbow in your mind. ROY-G-BIV. Imagine each color, starting with red, and hold that image in your mind for about 10 seconds. Then go to the next color. Practice taking deep, relaxing breaths as you imagine each color. Before you do this at night in bed, practice seeing the colors in your mind during the day.

If you cannot easily see the colors then imagine a bowl of fruit that has each of these delicious treats - apple, orange, banana, kiwi, blueberry, blackberry, grape. Each of these fruits coincides with a color of the rainbow.

Start with the color red (apple).

Slowly breathe in and out.

Imagine the color orange (orange).

Slowly breathe in and out.

Imagine the color yellow (banana).

Slowly breathe in and out.

Imagine the color green (kiwi).

Slowly breathe in and out.

Imagine the color blue (blueberry).

Slowly breathe in and out.

Imagine the color indigo (blackberry).

Slowly breathe in and out.

Imagine the color violet (purple grape).

Slowly breathe in and out.

Now, imagine yourself sinking down into the comfort of the fluffy white cloud at the end of the rainbow. Float away in peaceful sleep.

(END of Visualization)

When you first try this visualization, you might not be able to go instantly to sleep. Just bring your mind back to the image of the fluffy cloud. Keep imagining the cloud and sinking down into the fluffy softness. You will soon be able to float away. I can use this imagery and fall asleep without any problems now. If you have trouble, just try again the next night. Do not worry about it. Just try again tomorrow. I have taught this technique successfully to many people, and I know that you can do it, too!

Indigo is the deepest, darkest blue of a midnight sky. And I always see violet as that shade of purple in the night sky as the sun is setting. By the time you get to violet, you will be ready to imagine floating away on a cloud surrounded by a lovely violet light. That is a moment of true peace.

You can even use this visualization to help you get back to sleep in the middle of the night. If you have a nightmare or need to get up to pee (because you did not limit your liquids before going to bed – I told you so….) then just go back through all the colors of the rainbow and float off again on that fluffy cloud.

CHAPTER THEMES:

Insomnia

Sleep Medication

Logical Conclusions

Bedtime Guidelines for Adults

Rainbow Visualization

CHAPTER 11: NIGHTMARES

"Do not look at the external world as your enemy.
Your greatest enemy is within. Your greatest
strength and power is, too!"

NIGHTMARES ONCE WERE a tremendous problem for me. I lived through so much anxiety when I was raising my son. We were dealing with so much stress due to his medical condition. And when my husband abandoned us and turned instead to drugs, it left me destitute and alone. It was truly a time of anxiety. Nightmares plagued me during many of those years.

When my son was very young, I had a recurring nightmare. I had conquered it through meditation, exercise, and working on my sleep habits. When my son was in his early teens, we were in a serious car wreck. Then later that same year, he was in another traumatic accident. The physical trauma triggered more emotional stress and trauma. That can happen. Your emotions can be affected by problems with the physical body, and the physical body can be affected by emotional problems. That happened in full force to me.

The two accidents happened over one summer. The nightmare I had battled and thought I had conquered, returned to plague me. It was debilitating. It was the reason I had to consult with a specialist. Dr. Joanne Davis and her team at the University of Tulsa, in Tulsa, Oklahoma, created a program which she calls "Exposure, Relaxation and Rescripting Therapy (ERRT)." They are experts on researching and treating trauma-related nightmares. This program worked for me. And it gave me a fabulous tool for dealing with nightmares.

In the nightmare, I am swimming with my young son in a deep ocean area that is just about ten feet from shore. My subconscious placed me in a very frightening environment in the dream with the most frightening creature I know of – a great white shark. In the dream, I am trying to keep us afloat while trying to get to shore. I can see the shark coming for us. But then I realize it is coming for my child. The shark is coming for my son like a torpedo from the deep.

I kick at it and yell at it and try my best to make it leave while I am dragging us to shore. It is stronger and faster than I am. We are in the shark's element. It savages my son and then swims away. I drag my little boy onto the shore. He is dying right before my eyes.

He tells me, "Mommy, I am so cold." I hold him and tell him that all he has to do is close his eyes. I will hold him and keep him warm. He asks me, "Mommy, am I dying?" And I tell him, "Yes, sweetie, you are. But I am right here, and I will be with you every moment. Just close your eyes and I will sing you a song." I always wake up crying right there at that moment, with a song on my lips and a dying child in my arms.

That nightmare was brutal and savage. I knew exactly what it meant. It does not take a therapist to explain. Yes, in real life we were fighting a deadly enemy – his medical disorders. And yes, in real life, I had held him in my arms plenty of times while he nearly died. He even remembers the time he was in the end stages of anaphylaxis and his heart stopped. That is brutal for a child to remember and know and think about their own death.

The nightmare was not hard to figure out. What was hard to figure out was WHY it kept returning to plague me. Why? Why did it show up when I was under the most stress? What sort of crappy, cosmic game was my brain playing with me?

After reading all the self-help information I could find and doing hours of research, I had the beginnings of an answer. Think of your brain as having soft, spongy grooves or pathways. Each thought travels on a groove, a neural pathway, as the synapses are firing and the chemicals transferring the messages in your brain.

If you think a thought often enough, obsessing over and over, you might make a permanent groove in your brain for that thought. You have millions, no BILLIONS, of grooves in your brain. This is how you can have a thought just come up in your mind without thinking about it. Have you ever had a thought pop into your mind? Now, have you ever had a recurring thought pop into your mind, over and over?

Some people have recurring thoughts that annoy and frighten them. Some thoughts are just junk. And if you think a junk thought, or focus on trashy thoughts, then you are more likely to have more of those types of thoughts pop into your head. This is why it is important to safeguard your thoughts. Personally, I do not listen, watch, or read negative things. (Or else my head would be filled with negativity.) You can think yourself into a negative state. And can think yourself into a positive one. Just work hard to create good thoughts and good grooves in your brain.

When the body is asleep, the brain goes through cycles. At some point, it is processing memories, thoughts, ideas, and subconscious urgings. It is on auto-pilot. That is why nightmares can be so devastating. My theory is that your brain is actually trying to help you during a nightmare. It is taking the worst thoughts and trying to make sense of them to process and get rid of them.

Many people who have experienced trauma suffer from nightmares. Some issues like rape, molestation, death, and illness create tremendous amounts of stress in the mind. Those things are so frightening they will show up in nightmares quite often, even for people who have not experienced them.

It makes sense that my mind would be trying to deal with the possibility of my son's death. He is at the mercy of an awful disorder that we cannot control. My brain was trying to process all that stress and help me. I found a way to help my brain process all those images during the night.

When I spoke with Dr. Davis about this book, she was excited to know that I would be sharing this information with you. She had one issue for me to mention – this program is more effective at first when done with a therapist than when someone tries to tackle it alone. And that makes total sense to me! It helps to have someone guide you when you are dealing with one of the most frightening aspects of your subconscious or sleeping mind. Nightmares are terrifying.

So please visit her website and read all about how their team is leading the way in helping trauma survivors with nightmares! That website is in the

Resources section at the end of the book, along with all sorts of other useful information.

You meet once a week with a therapist for four or five weeks. Each session lasts about ninety minutes. There are four main parts to the therapy. First you learn about nightmares, trauma, sleeping habits, and relaxation. You finish with writing exercises and talking about the nightmares.

Now when I wake up from a nightmare or if I remember one in the morning, I write it down quickly. I keep a journal by the bed just for this. The next day I rewrite the nightmare. I change the outcome and make it a kinder, gentler nightmare. Take a shark and make it a teddy bear. Or make it a minnow. Or change the ocean into a bathtub and the shark into a rubber ducky. I make it funny and happy and get rid of the scary parts.

When I go to bed that night, I read the new, kinder, gentler dream aloud. And if I wake up with that nightmare, I at once stop and tell myself "No! That is not the way it goes." I think of the new dream with the new ending and go back to sleep. Eventually, I got to the point where I could manage the nightmares easily.

I have not had horrible, recurring nightmares in years now! That is amazing. If I ever do have another nightmare, then I know how to handle it. My sleep is more peaceful. I get more rest. My brain is back to processing regular life instead of creating nightmares to process the trauma.

Even during the weeks and months after my husband died, I was able to keep the nightmares away and have restful sleep. I think that when you experience tragedy and trauma, it is even more important to have positive coping skills already in place. It definitely was for me! Because I had been using all these skills I write about in this book, I was able to process the grief, and heal my broken heart.

My sleep is better now, but my mornings are still difficult. I am not a morning person. Morning people are happy and annoying. I say that with love, because my new husband IS a morning person. He wakes up happy. I have to remind myself to be happy just to wake up. And I have to remind him to leave me alone until I am fully caffeinated. (And please pardon my irritation if you ARE a morning person!) Thankfully, I have found other ways to make my mornings better.

CHAPTER THEMES:

Nightmares

Physical and Emotional Trauma

Brains with Grooves

Neural Pathways

Dr. Joanne Davis

ERRT Therapy

Rescripting

CHAPTER 12:
THE MOST IMPORTANT
MINUTE OF THE DAY

"When you sleep an average of 8 hours a night, you have 960 wakeful minutes every day. That is 960 chances each day to make life better."

THE FIRST MINUTE YOU WAKE UP can set the emotional and psychological tone for your entire day. I believe it is the single most important minute of the day. And it is the single most difficult minute of mine. There are several ways to start your day. Some people exercise, some people pray or meditate, some people have a cup of coffee. All of that is great. But before I even get out of bed, I have a life-changing routine in place.

I have never been a morning person. The worst part is those few minutes when the brain shifts from sleep to wake. For me it is more than just being grumpy in the morning. It takes a couple of hours for me to feel real. I am not fully awake until about 10 am each morning. I joke about this with my husband, telling him to leave me alone until I get a cup of tea. (Or two.)

I use all the good sleep practices we have discussed - like going to bed at a routine time, limiting my caffeine or food intake several hours before bed, and re-scripting my nightmares. Even with all that the mornings are still awful!

What I have never shared until now is how depressed I feel every morning. It is the most dangerous time of the day for me. For my thoughts. It is the bleakest time when my inner critic is brutal and mean.

Fear, nightmares, depression, and chemical imbalances - those were all part of my pattern of thought and behavior. They were also part of a pattern of suicidal ideation. People do not like to talk about suicide. Well, too bad. We need to talk about it! If you or someone you love is thinking about suicide, call the National Suicide Prevention Hotline right now - it is open 24 hours a day - 1-800-273-8255.

The thought of suicide was like a release valve for me. After living through so much stress and trauma, my mind would create this idea that…. well, I always have the choice to kill myself. Remember in the last chapter, we discussed the pathways in the brain for thoughts. When you think a thought often enough you make a pathway in your brain for it. If you actively think a thought often enough then it will sometimes just pop into your mind all on its own. That is how I became plagued with suicidal ideas.

Just because you have an idea form in your brain, that does not mean it is a good one. Sometimes you have junk images, ideas, and thoughts in your brain.

That is what suicidal ideas are! They are freaking junk thoughts.

If you actively think negative thoughts, then negative thoughts will show up in your mind. And if you actively think positive thoughts… do you see where I am headed with this? The idea that I have the "power of choice" for destruction is quite a negative thought. What if I turned that around and made a positive "power of choice" thought instead?

I am prepared EVERY morning to combat my negative, inner dialog. I make a total "Attitude Adjustment." I started doing this over 20 years ago. When my son was a toddler, the reality of his medical problems had begun taking a toll on my mental health. After we made it through the first few years of his life, I fully understood that he had a life-long condition. I would have to readjust to the reality of having a chronically sick child. And I would have to teach him the same thing.

Life is difficult when you have chronic illness. Some illnesses (and some situations) will never go away. They must be managed but are never cured. That is what happened with me and my son. That brings its own set of stresses. So, I began meditating in earnest. And I developed the practice of GRATITUDE! For me, gratitude is not an emotion that is fleeting and felt only when you open up a gift or someone does you a favor. Gratitude is an emotional state that I actively practice each day. And I practice it each morning through my "Attitude Adjustment." It is also a part of my life and practice as a Reiki Master.

And here is how I do it. I start off every morning with stretches in bed. I rotate my ankles and wrists just to get my joints limber. While my body is waking and stretching, so is my mind. With my eyes still closed I consciously focus on breathing in the divine forces of good and breathing out any tension or bad thoughts. It might take me three deep breaths, or it might take ten. Whatever it takes!

Then I sit up on the side of my bed and begin my Attitude Adjustment! Now, there are usually a few negative thoughts in my head each morning. (Remember – I am not a morning person!) There may be some left-over images from a dream or just some junk thought that is roaming around in my brain. I decided to combat each and every negative thought when it showed up in the mornings.

I told each negative thought to go away and I chose the positive instead. After a while, I started seeing a few patterns. Several emotions and thoughts showed up again and again throughout the years. They were: worry, anger, weakness/passivity, selfishness and sorrow. I got tired of them hanging around and bugging me. There are now five positive attributes I focus on and claim each morning instead.

When I am finally ready to stand up and start my day, I stretch again. I stand up in the Wonder Woman power pose (I am totally serious here) and then I focus on these five thoughts:

From Worried to HOPEFUL,

From Angry to FULL of LOVE,

From Passive to ACTIVE,

From Selfish to FULL of KINDNESS,

From Sad to GRATEFUL.

These are the personal statements I make every morning. I claim these attributes aloud! These are my goals for every day. This is my daily Attitude Adjustment. I choose to think positive, uplifting thoughts because I choose to be a positive, uplifting person. I do this for ME. No one else can change your attitude. ONLY YOU CAN.

Just a note here about the Wonder Woman power pose. Social scientist Amy Cuddy shared a brilliant TED talk about power poses. You can find it online. Just search for "TED Talks" and "Amy Cuddy." Her presentation is titled: "Your body language may shape who you are."

You have seen depressed people who are slumped over and their shoulders are hanging down. Their head is hanging low. Body language and non-verbal communication often shows someone's mental state. Well, Amy Cuddy theorizes that you can decrease your stress hormones (cortisol) and increase your feel-good hormones by assuming a positive, upright physical position.

Try it! For 60 seconds, stand like Wonder Woman or Super Man. Stand up with your feet spread apart and your hands on your hips. Chest out, shoulders back, chin held high.

I do this every morning. Thankfully, there is no one around except my hubby to see me standing in my fuzzy slippers and nightgown while striking my power pose! While I am striking that pose, I am also going through my "Attitude Adjustment." I know it might sound weird, but it works. (In my seminars, we practice the power poses!) Try it tomorrow morning. It will make the first minute of your morning the most important and positive minute of your entire day.

And here is your first bit of homework in our book! I want you to think of the attitude, feeling, or emotion that you want to change. You will also need to find the one you want to claim instead. Find one word that best describes the feeling you want to change.   Make at least one word-pair. Do not overwhelm yourself by trying to work on too much. Just choose one or two that are the most important for you to change right now. Get a piece of paper or your notebook and a pen.

Use this example:

"From _____ to _____."

To help you jump start the thinking process, try this word list:

able

active

accepting

adaptable

alone

angry

afraid

attractive

balanced

bold

brave

calm

caring

cheerful

clever

compassionate

confident

conflicted

content

critical

dependable

depressed

empathetic

energetic

extroverted

fearful

friendly

free

flexible

giving

grateful

guilty

grumpy

gossipy

happy

helpful

hopeful

hopeless

independent

introverted

irritable

kind

knowledgeable

lonely

loving

mature

messy

modest

nervous

organized

outgoing

optimistic

passive

passionate

patient

powerful

relaxed

resentful

responsive

resilient

sad

self-assertive

self-conscious

sensible

shy

supportive

sympathetic

tense

trusting

trustworthy

unloved

unsure

warm

weak

wise

worthless

Make up your mind that you will make at least one positive mental change every morning. I have five of them now but remember that I did not start off with all five at once! The first one I started with was "SAD." And instead I claimed "GRATEFUL." You cannot be sad when you are feeling grateful. You cannot be whining about what you do not have when you are so thankful for what you do have.

You are making a new pathway in your brain for a positive thought. Remember that some negative thoughts are just junk. And our goal is to help the brain! The brain processes all sorts of negatives that you read, hear and speak. Start off each morning with a positive statement. You claim it, and it will be so. Be Wonder Woman or Super Man. Claim it every day.

Just in case your mornings are too hectic to do this, pick another time that works for you. Afternoon or evening might be better for you than in the morning. Maybe your inner negative voices are worse in the afternoon. Use your new word-pairs when they will help YOU the most.

Soon that "new" part of you will blossom and grow. Print off your word-pairs and place them beside your bed so you can read it the first thing in the morning. I do this every day for ME! It is my daily Attitude Adjustment.

CHAPTER THEMES:

First Minute of the Day

Suicidal Ideation

Junk Ideas

Attitude Adjustment

Word-Pairs

Wonder Woman Pose

Amy Cuddy/TED Talks

CHAPTER 13: ATTITUDE IS EVERYTHING!

"It can sometimes be hard to stay positive when you look around at all the misery in the world. Of course, that is when it is most important to keep your heart open to love and life!"

SO, DO POSITIVE AFFIRMATIONS WORK? Does it really matter whether you keep a positive attitude? Yes, it does. You can go back thousands of years to various holy scriptures that tell you to think on positive things. Here though, is my favorite saying about positive thinking:

- Keep your thoughts positive because your thoughts become your words.
- Keep your words positive because your words become your behavior.
- Keep your behavior positive because your behavior becomes your habits.
- Keep your habits positive because your habits become your values.
- Keep your values positive because your values become your destiny.

These beautiful quotes are from Mahatma Gandhi, the Indian political and spiritual leader. This is the perfect explanation for WHY we should focus on positive thoughts. It is the bedrock of a better life. Positive thoughts lead to a positive destiny!

So how do you use positive affirmations to help shape your life? At the end of the book, in Bonus Chapter #2, there is a list with 100 Positive

Affirmations. Find 7-10 of them that you really like, the ones that really speak to you. Write them on notecards or print them out on a sheet of paper OR write them in lipstick on your bathroom mirror. Just find a way to keep one of them in front of you each day!

I am a fan of Zig Ziglar, Jim Rohn and Napoleon Hill! If you do not know about their writings, then I would recommend that you go immediately to the nearest computer and google them. Their combined writings keep me motivated on a daily basis. I have a motivational board in my office. Each of these men are represented on my wall. Because each of them knew this secret: your attitude is more important that your intellect! It is more important than your abilities! It is the most important aspect of your success in anything!

Your dedicated belief that you CAN battle stress, you CAN rise up after trauma, you CAN change your life, you CAN make it better – is the absolute deciding factor in whether you will or you will not. Whether you believe you can or you believe you cannot, you are correct.

On one of my Facebook business pages (Success with Shanna and Mark) I have a running MasterMind club that is all about Napoleon Hill's writings. His writings are over a hundred years old, and can be a bit difficult for the modern reader to follow. But great ideas stand the test of time!

Zig Ziglar had a funny saying about motivation, *"People often say that motivation doesn't last. Well neither does bathing – that's why we recommend it daily."* OMG.

And how about this one from Jim Rohn, *"We must all wage an intense, lifelong battle against the downward pull. If we relax, the bugs and weeds of negativity will move into the garden and take away everything of value."*

Ah, these sayings guide my life and have helped me get through so many tough times. And as a mom, a daughter, a sister, an aunt, and a spouse, I try to share positive words with the people I love. (That now includes you, dear reader.)

And one of my favorite stories about positive attitude comes directly from an experience I had with my son. About nine years ago, we experienced one of the toughest years ever. It had nothing to do with anaphylaxis or depression. It had everything to do with two separate freak accidents. We lived through a year of physical trauma. That causes emotional trauma, too.

My son and I were in a horrible car wreck. My side of the car was crumpled and the impact spun us around several times. My legs took the main hit. My door was crushed in and I could not get out. The police and ambulance got there quickly. There were three cars involved, two were totaled, including ours.

Thankfully, my son did not have anything broken. Neither did I. But everyone went to the hospital. I developed a huge hematoma on my left leg where the glove box hit me with blunt force trauma.

The wound never healed. Instead, it started decaying from the inside and developed compartment syndrome. I had to have surgery to remove all the decaying tissue, and was left with a huge wound in my leg. A huge chunk of muscle tissue from the right, front part of my leg was removed, all the way down to the tendons. (I still have a huge divot in my leg, and the nerve endings have never recovered.) They hooked me up to a wound pump to speed the healing. I would need nursing and home health care visits for several months.

I dragged that medical device around all summer while my body healed. I had to drag it to another hospital later that summer when my son had another freak accident. He was helping my brother move a refrigerator down at my Mom's house. The fridge slipped, and my son's hand was slit open. He had work gloves on or he might have lost his hand. He told me that it didn't hurt at first. It felt like a hard hit, but he didn't realize he was slit open until he saw all the blood.

He had been through so many emergencies that he knew to remain calm. He sat down and held the wound closed while trying to limit the bleeding. I got the phone call and we headed to the little rural hospital with the emergency lights flashing all the way. We were 60 miles away but we beat the ambulance. Hey, I was a motivated mom!

The nurses and doctors got him stabilized and stitched up the gaping wound. But there was nothing more they could do. The wound was too deep and severe. My kiddo was pumped full of pain medicine, but it did not really help. One of the hardest things I ever did as his Mom was to sit with him in that exam room and tell him that I totally believed it was fixable. I was staring down into his sliced-open hand looking at his tendons moving. The wound started up by the index finger and continued down past his wrist. He was lucky to still have a thumb attached. The cut had barely missed the main artery. Out in a rural setting, he could have bled out before the ambulance even made it there. He had emergency surgery the next morning at a big hospital with a great hand surgeon.

We were now both physically wounded with the scars to prove it. We also have the emotional scars that you cannot see. Every trauma, physical or not, causes pain. He developed some PTSD symptoms and did not drive for a year after our car accident. I knew that the longer it took for him to get back into a vehicle and drive, the harder it would get. When I helped him finally face his fear of driving, we went to THAT intersection. He drove and I was his passenger and we lived through it. Facing your fears is often the only way to conquer them.

It has been nine years since the accidents and we both have nerve damage in our respective scars. I am lucky to still have my left leg and he is lucky he can still play video games with both thumbs!

There was one moment with my son several months after his hand accident that I will always cherish. His girlfriend had mentioned to him that he must have awful luck going through two serious accidents in just a few months. He walked into the kitchen one afternoon and quietly asked me if I thought he had "bad luck." I knew my teenager had something serious going on in his head when he voluntarily wanted to talk to me. I calmly asked him instead what HE thought. He told me what his girlfriend said. He felt the total opposite of her, he felt like he had good luck!

"Just think, Mom," he told me, "someone could have died, or I could have really lost my thumb. It could have been much, much worse. I think that is pretty lucky!"

I calmly agreed with him and gave him a huge hug. He grabbed a snack - which is probably why he really came to the kitchen in the first place - and meandered back to his room to play more video games.

Attitude is the most important part of success in anything. It is more important that your intellect! It is more important than your abilities! A positive attitude will get you through horrible situations and help you rise, no matter what. A positive attitude looks at the bad in life and decides that it will CHOOSE to see something, it will CHOOSE to find something good in the midst of the bad.

After talking with my son, on the inside I was doing a happy dance! I knew then that my son was a success story. He can look at his life, with all the stress and turmoil, the doctor visits, medicines and disease, and yet still recognize those moments of grace. He KNOWS to look for and value the good and to find it wherever he can. He knows how blessed he truly is.

I taught him that!

CHAPTER THEMES:

Positive Affirmations

Master Mind Group

Physical Trauma

Emotional Trauma

Facing Problems

Bad Luck?

Attitude is Everything

CHAPTER 14: RESISTANCE AND YOUR INNER CRITIC

"Do not be afraid of your negative emotions. They are there to teach you a lesson. They are there to show you that something needs to change."

I AM NOT EXACTLY SURE HOW to introduce this topic to you. It is important for you to know about, but it is difficult to explain. I am sure there is a code or designation in psychotherapy for this issue. Doctors and therapists have all sorts of ways to describe this aspect of personal growth. I have just always thought of it as the "downside of the upside."

I am sure you know someone who is never happy unless others are miserable. It could be your best friend. (Then please get a new one.) It could be a family member like your parents or siblings. For me it was a grandmother. She delighted in knowing and hearing bad news. She was not a horrible person, and she did not look down on others when bad things happened to them. It just confirmed her belief that the world was awful.

The negative things in her life and in other people's lives she saw as the dominant outcome of life itself. She was not a happy person. Other people were unhappy around her, including her sons. Unhappiness breeds more unhappiness. (Always remember that the opposite is also true: happiness shared leads to more happiness.)

This attitude of looking at the exterior world as negative can lead to all sorts of problems. When something good came along in her life she would say,

"Well, this won't last." She assumed that something bad was just around the corner even when something good was right in front of her!

In her later years she developed a slow-growing cancer. It was not invasive, and the doctor told her it would not kill her. She might need some treatments for it eventually, but even that was easy to do and not a problem. If you had to get cancer, this was the kind to get!

Instead of being happy that the cancer would not kill her, her outlook remained negative. She came away from the doctor's appointment with the mindset that she was not valued enough as a human being to be treated right then and there for her cancer. She took the good news and made it bad! This mindset that looks for the bad even in the middle of the good is present inside you, too. It is not just in the minds of little grandmas who lived through the Great Depression.

At times it is easier to go back to old patterns of behavior and thought than it is to make new patterns of behavior and thought. Changing your life is hard! Changing your behavior and your thoughts takes tremendous effort.

There will be times when you look at all the good in your life and instead you will see bad. You will look at the good things you have created, and you will say, "This won't last." This resistance to positive change exists in everyone! It is far easier to stay miserable or addicted or negative or sad, than it is to get up and make changes. I know. I have struggled with this issue many times. It is the bad thing about making things better; it is the "downside of the upside."

When you start making changes in any aspect of your life this resistance to change will pop up. Your mind will throw up all sorts of reasons to NOT change. Your inner dialog will tell you that it will not last, that it is not worth it, that nothing will be better in the end.

SHUT THAT INNER CRITIC DOWN! Anytime your inner negative voice starts talking smack, tell it to stop. Be prepared. Have a list of the positive reasons for making changes. And I mean this literally – make a list. Keep it on your phone or in your purse or pocket. Bring it out and read it often to silence the negative voice in your head. Always remember your WHY.

Remember how I told you about exercise being one of the most important things I do to help myself and my brain? Every time I exercise, I battle my inner critic. My inner voice does not want me to exercise; it does not want me to make the effort. My inner voice tells me to eat bon-bons! I know exercise is good for me and I know I will feel good afterwards, but I still must battle the inner resistance to change.

As you work hard to make positive changes in your life you will find that resistance from your inner critic will grow. You may also find that the outer critics will grow, too.

My grandmother made other people unhappy. The problem was not just her own personal dialog making her think negative thoughts. She shared that negativity with the people around her. She spread it around.

Watch out for the people who are closest to you and their voices of negativity. It might come from the ones who you think should support you the most – your siblings and parents, or your spouse. If your closest relationships make you miserable, then change the ones that you can. Be strong in your desire to make personal changes and your conviction that you can.

Silence the critics. You might not be able to stop them from talking negatively. But you can stop listening to them. Most people will eventually come around and support you. Remember, they are not strong like you are. They may not even realize how hateful they are. They may not know about their own inner critic and how to shut it down. This is where you get to hold up a candle in the dark. You get to show and teach the people around you about how to make positive changes. As they see you grow and see you actively making your life better it will inspire them, too.

There is a wonderful book about this issue in my recommended reading section. It is "Balcony People" by Joyce Heatherley. There are two types of people in your life: balcony people and basement people.

Balcony people have a splendid view of life from above. They are shouting words of encouragement down to you on your journey. And they make you feel better about all those positive changes in your life. "Come on, you can do it. I am here for you!" That is the message from the balcony people.

The basement people just want you to come back down into the lower levels. You know what they are shouting at you. "Who do you think you are? Get back down here. You cannot do that." Many times, people in your own family are still in the basement. They are the negative, nay-sayers that want to bring you down. They do it with "good" intentions - they just want you to be realistic or understand what their idea of reality is. Phooey on that.

Find your balcony people. You might not be able to end all your relationships with the basement-dwellers, but you can balance them out with balcony people. I will be a balcony person for you. Seriously. Send me an email. Join my mailing list and we will chat.

Just a word of warning here. It is not all sunshine and lollipops! Keeping a positive attitude is different than ignoring the issues. I am fully aware of the difficulties of life. I have experienced enough heartbreak and I know how awful people can be. And yet I still have a positive attitude. Because I CHOOSE so. You can do the same.

What is your most difficult part of the day? When do you have the most trouble with your inner critic? Remember the word-pair statements you made in the last chapter? That is now your "Attitude Adjustment." Use it when you need it. Be prepared for the battle with your inner critic – and the outer ones, too.

CHAPTER THEMES:

Resistance to Positive Change

Downside of the Upside

Negative People

Your Inner Critic

Basement People

Balcony People

CHAPTER 15:
WHAT ELSE CAN YOU
DO RIGHT NOW?

"Small choices can change your life in big ways. Be
mindful of how you spend your time, because one
moment could be an opportunity for setting up
future happiness."

THIS CHAPTER MAY BE SHORT, but it is full of
great ideas. We are taking a little break, because in
the next few chapters it will get a bit more intense.
We will be doing some difficult and life-changing
work in those chapters. I wanted to make sure you
had some simple activities that you can do right now.

Sometimes, when you start making BIG changes in your life, you might need to take a break and focus on something easier and lighter.

But do not discount this chapter just because it is small. These ten great ideas can make your life better. All of them are easy and quick to do. And they do not cost a penny. Sometimes it is the little steps we take each day that add up to substantial changes! I could write a book about each of the items on this list. And who knows, I might just do that. So, here are ten things you can do RIGHT NOW, to feel happier with your life.

1. Make a prayer/meditation area. I have candles and things from nature. I find bird feathers, pinecones and seashells. These things comfort me. Find what comforts you. Print out a favorite scripture or poem and hang it by your meditation space. I have a music player nearby so I can play a guided meditation or something

from my favorite composer. Music and relaxation go hand-in-hand.

2. Pick up the phone and call a non-toxic friend. And if all your friends are toxic, then make new ones. I have had to end some friendships because they were negative. You must protect yourself. Find positive people to hang out with. Or call your mom or a family member that really loves you. And tell them how much they mean to you. That will just spread the love around!

3. Reading a great book is a fabulous way to expand your mind and chill out. Find the stories that motivate you. Find the people who have risen above and succeeded and do what they did! Go check out my Top 10 Reading List for some recommendations. If you do not have time or the desire to read a book, then find a

positive, uplifting blog or podcast to follow. (Follow my blog at: www.shannawarner.com. My podcast is called: Natural Awakenings, and you can find it on Anchor, Spotify or iTunes, etc.)

4. Focus on someone else! It is easy to get wrapped up in your own issues. We all do this. Remembering that there are other people less fortunate than yourself can help you forget your own problems for a while. Visit a soup kitchen for the homeless or go volunteer at a school or nursing home. When my son and I started thinking we were poor, we would drive to the homeless shelter and remember how to be grateful! That is a terrific way to stop any pity-party.

5. Have a pampering afternoon! Take a bubble bath, paint your toenails, color your hair. Even

better is to partner up with your best friend and paint each other's toenails. Pop some corn, put on a great movie and pick out a hot, new color that makes you happy. Treat yourself well! Everyone deserves a little TLC. As you begin feeling better on the inside make sure your outside matches. People will notice. They will ask what you are doing to look so good.

6. Find people to fellowship with. This is vital! Find a support or hobby group. It does not have to be an abuse or trauma support group. It is all about balance in your life. You cannot always focus on fixing stuff, sometimes you must let go and have some fun. You love to knit? Find a group of happy knitters to be friends with. Or join a hiking group or a museum group. Or if you love to yodel then

find those other happy yodelers. (I know you yodelers are out there somewhere!)

7. Make a list of the things you want to give up or change in your life. Take some time and list those pains and frustrations. Yes, I understand this could be a huge list. But just focus on the here and now, make it one page of the changes you want to see in your life right now. Then BURN IT! Burn the list and scatter the ashes into the four winds. There is some serious freedom in this activity. It is a visual symbol of your desire for inner change.

8. Now, make a list of the things you want to gain or develop in your life! But do not burn this list. Get some crayons or markers or stickers and get creative! Make it beautiful. Art is therapy. It is okay if your artwork looks more like a toddler did it than Picasso or Van Gogh.

If it is really lovely, you could take the next step and laminate it. Or just put it on the wall beside your bed or on the mirror in your bathroom so you see it each day. Keeping that list of your goals and dreams in front of you is powerful inspiration!

9. Name the negatives. Practice some deep breathing and then write down what makes you afraid or embarrassed or angry. Take some time and make it complete. Now, add to the list the things you need to forgive yourself for. I think that often we are our own worst critic. We focus on something we did wrong and then dwell on that mistake. Well, cut that out! Forgive yourself and forgive others. This is one of the best, first ways to face issues. WRITE. Then rip that entire page up or burn it and scatter those ashes, too.

10. Download a positive, uplifting app on your phone. Set it to send you a message each day. I get a positive message twice a day, at 10am and at 2pm. (For me, that is teatime and coffee time, respectively.) If for some reason you do not have a phone, then go to the list of 100 Affirmations (in the Bonus chapter at the end of the book) and read one of them each day. That will get you through 3 months of positive messages. The goal is to just make sure that you feed your mind with a positive, uplifting message every day.

CHAPTER THEMES:

Small but Mighty

Little Changes

10 Great Ideas

CHAPTER 16:
STOP THE NEGATIVE
SELF-TALK

"Stop being so negative about yourself. Okay, you are not perfect. Sure, you have faults. But balance that out by knowing your strengths and your awesome abilities!"

WE ARE GOING TO DISCUSS whether your thoughts and beliefs are helping or hurting, if they are positive or negative, if they are making your life better or worse. Negative beliefs are where negative self-talk begins. This is an assumption or a belief that you might have about yourself, others or just life in general. These beliefs can be damaging and wrong.

Where do they come from? Usually we learn these beliefs from our family or from society. We judge others, almost always negatively. We cast judgement on our family members, on people we do not even know, on people we see on television. All this judgement causes negative thoughts and beliefs. But who is the biggest judge of your own life? YOU are.

You may not even know that you have such beliefs deep inside your mind. But you do. We all do. Here is an example of negative self-talk that you might have said yourself or heard someone else say. I call it the "Duh-factor."

How many times have you made a mistake and said, either aloud or to yourself, "Geez, I'm so stupid," or maybe, "I always make that mistake," or "I just can't figure this out," or some other negative statement that you make about yourself. Or you hit your forehead and said, "DUH!"

When my son was growing up, we had a "No-Duh" rule in the house. Do not ever "DUH" yourself! You do not get to say bad things to or about yourself. You do not get to cut yourself down. Life is hard enough without you becoming your own worst enemy. Make this a fixed rule for you and your loved ones!

Your tongue is the strongest muscle in the body. You can hurt someone to the core with your negative words. And that someone might just be yourself. Start listening to what you say. Start listening to your own inner dialogue. There are plenty of negative beliefs floating around in your head. Think back to a time when you said something negative. I bet there is an inner negative belief behind the outer negative statement.

A statement based on negative beliefs would sound something like this...

"My life is just too hard."

"Things do not work out for people like me."

"If I could just get a break."

"No one understands me."

"People just do not care about me."

"All I have is bad luck."

"They will just laugh at me."

"Everything is going to hell."

"You cannot trust anyone these days."

"I did not get a degree, so I cannot succeed."

"I just do not have the energy."

"There are no good men (women) left."

These types of negative beliefs about life and the world in general will create more stress and anxiety. Or it can make existing depression even worse. Every negative thought holds you back from higher awareness and growth. Becoming aware of them and choosing to change these beliefs will lead to a better life. You are capable of clearing your mind of this negativity and self-judgement. You will be less stressed out, less worried, and happier. Can you see how a negative belief can lead to negative self-talk? This can be a very deep and destructive habit.

If you believe the world is dangerous and no one is to be trusted, then when someone helps you out you will be ungrateful and untrusting. You might not even remember to say "Thank you." Instead, you will wonder what their motivations are. You will assume the negative.

Have you ever denied a compliment? This is a common example of a negative belief leading to negative statements. When someone gives you a genuine compliment do you counter it with a negative statement? Someone says to you, "oh that _____ was wonderful." And you say, "Oh, it wasn't that good." Some sort of negative thinking stops you from accepting a genuine compliment. Start listening closely to other people and you will hear statements based on their negative personal beliefs, too.

A statement based on negative *personal* beliefs would sound like this....

"I cannot do that."

"I have no talent."

"I do not know how."

"I am not smart."

"I am not pretty like she is."

"I always screw things up."

"It just takes too much time."

"I cannot figure this out."

"It just takes too much energy."

"I will probably fail anyway."

"I do not deserve it."

And here we get to the very heart of the problem. "I do not deserve it." These negative, deep-seated beliefs are usually based on some skewed idea about self-worth. The idea that your worth is dependent on some external factor, like wealth, social status, the type of home you have, the car you drive, or love from someone else (parents, spouse, etc.) is a deep-seated one. Our society and our families reinforce this notion that WORTH is based on external factors like money and social status.

Think of the many times you have heard someone who gets public assistance described in a negative way. They are being judged on social status. And there are many, many people and families who just need a little help to keep food on the table or gas in the car. They need help so they can rise! That does not mean they are worth less than someone with a fat bank account.

There are so many ways that society divides us. From the color of our skin to the size of our bank accounts, we are constantly judged by someone else's standard, society's standards, political and religious standards, external standards. Children are socialized and take all this judgement in from the time they are born.

When your self-worth is external it prevents you from realizing just how many great qualities you have down deep in your own soul. Self-worth needs to be internal! You can learn to respect and believe in yourself. You do this by first recognizing where you are getting those mistaken messages about your worth and value as a human being. Remind yourself that this may be how you feel at the moment, but this is not where you will stay. You choose to identify and get rid of the negativity. As you begin listening and identifying those negative, judgmental statements and beliefs, just remind yourself that you are part of the Divine nature of the universe!

We all have developed mistaken beliefs. You heard messages as a child from parents, school, or church that you have now internalized. Here is a destructive statement that too many children hear: "You will never amount to anything when you grow up." If a child hears negative statements often enough, then they will sink to that level. The negative statement becomes a self-fulfilling prophecy that follows them into adulthood.

As adults, we need to talk realistically and kindly to children. They need to be corrected with love when they make mistakes. But never demeaned. If we can do that for children, then we can do that for ourselves!

What are the negative beliefs that you have internalized? It is critical to uncover your own negative beliefs and reprogram the negative self-talk. Earlier you made word pairs for the morning routine of "Attitude Adjustment." We are going to continue that work now by writing out your negative belief statements. Then we will correct that belief with positive counterstatements.

When I help someone in a seminar with this work, I tell them to imagine the classic image of an Angel on one shoulder and a Devil on the other! The "Devil" will give you the negative, mistaken belief; the "Angel" will help you create and uncover the positive, uplifting counterstatement.

In one of my favorite books, Miguel Ruiz's *The Four Agreements,* he tells a story of a mother who came home from work one day with a tremendous headache. Her little girl was skipping around the house singing a happy song. Momma says to the child, "Please stop that. Your voice is so ugly." The child stops singing and never sings again. The child internalized the message that her voice was ugly. It was not ugly; mom was just having a horrible day. But the damage was done, whether the mother meant for the harm to happen or not.

Do you have an internalized moment of damage? It might not be a single moment. It might instead be a cluster of moments? Were you taught that you are less valuable because of the way you look? Or sound? Or believe? Did someone demean you and cause you to believe that you deserve less? Find that moment and let us work together to change it!

We are going to take a few minutes right now and write down some of those mistaken beliefs that you have about yourself. Get a pen and a piece of paper or your notebook. We will start re-writing your mistaken beliefs and make some counterstatements. This could be a little painful. It can be distressing to start realizing that society or your family gave you some negative beliefs. This little moment of pain can lead to some wonderful healing.

This is a deeply personal activity. No two people will have the same mistaken beliefs, although there might be some common threads. There may be one single false belief that you were given many years ago that is still holding you back, or there could be many. You can find freedom and begin to rewrite your life. I believe in transformation and this can be a transformative moment for you. Take time and write them down now!

My Mistaken Beliefs

1. _____

2. _____

3. _____

4. _____

5. _____

Now we are going to examine each of those mistaken beliefs. This is how we will begin to write counterstatements and start changing that negative belief today. For each of the mistaken beliefs you just wrote down, I want you to ask yourself some basic questions about that belief. Ask yourself:

- Where did this belief come from?
- Is this based on fact or is this someone's opinion?
- Is this belief harming me or holding me back?

Now, for each mistaken belief, write a counterstatement. Use those three questions as a guideline for inspiration! Remember the image of the Angel on one shoulder and the Devil on the other. Let the better Angels of your nature guide you to make those counterstatements.

My Counterstatements:

1. _____

2. _____

3. _____

4. _____

5. _____

Making statements and counterstatements is a wonderful way to find and correct the negative thinking in your brain. Come back to this activity in a day or so. You may find there are some more negative statements that pop up in your head overnight. You may remember some painful situations that caused deep-seated distress. This is good! When you find the negative, then you can change it.

Above all else, be kind and understanding of others and of yourself. Even when you find that family or society gave you negatives, remember that they just did not know better. Now YOU know better. You know that having a spark of the Divine in you means that you are worth it! You are worth all the energy and time it takes to make it better. It takes time and practice to change the negatives, just like it took time and practice to develop the judgmental habits. The more you remember to be loving and kind to yourself, the more loving and kind you will automatically be to others.

If you had trouble thinking of what to write, here are a few examples of negative, mistaken beliefs and the positive, counter statements.

Negative, Mistaken Belief - *"I am a victim. I have no power."* Positive, Counter Statement - *"No. I am a survivor. I DO have choices! I am in control of my choices. I am in control of my life right now. I can do this."*

Negative, Mistaken Belief - *"I cannot change anything. This is just the way it is."* Positive, Counter Statement - *"I may not be able to fix every problem I have, but I can fix my attitude. I choose to make positive changes."*

Negative, Mistaken Belief - *"I am a failure. I always will be. Why even try?"* Positive, Counter Statement – *"It is okay to fail sometimes. If I fail, then I will learn from that mistake and not make it again. I cannot grow if I do not try."*

Negative, Mistaken Belief - *"Life is awful, and it always will be."* Positive, Counter Statement - *"Life is an adventure. I will find something great today to enjoy. I will find something every day to enjoy. That is my choice."*

Negative, Mistaken Belief - *"I am not important to anyone."* Positive, Counter Statement - *"I am important to ME! I will be good to myself today. I will love myself today and spread that love around."*

If you want the changes to be more permanent, then you need to take the next 21 days and make your positive thinking into a new habit! You *can* reduce your stress. You *can* retrain your mind. You *can* recreate a more beneficial pathway. You *can* transform your thoughts.

CHAPTER THEMES:

Negative Self-Talk

Duh Factor

External/Internal Worth

Mistaken Beliefs

Internalized Messages

Changing the Message

CHAPTER 17:
21 VITAL QUESTIONS

"It takes time to make positive changes. Bad change can happen in an instant – like from car wrecks and tornadoes. Good change takes time, effort, and persistence!"

RIGHT NOW, YOU MIGHT BE thinking something along the lines of - *"Yeah, right, you are telling me that all I have to do is think happy thoughts and then everything turns into sunshine and lollipops? What a load of crap."* I truly wish it was that easy! If it was, there would be no reason for this book or any self-help book or doctors or therapists. But, no. There is more to it than just wishful thinking.

If I told you that in one month your life could be tremendously different, would you believe me? It is true. And that is the focus of this chapter. I want you to trust yourself. Trust in your ability to change. And take the time to listen, ask, ponder and know. These next three weeks will build upon everything you have read and experienced in this book so far.

It is all about choices and action. When you combine positive action with your new positive thoughts, then you have the beginnings of a new habit of positive change! If you have an attitude that you WILL make positive changes and you WILL take positive action, then that is what will make the difference. Your future is formed in the thinking of the here and now! We will literally become what we think about, so make sure you are focused on the positive and uplifting. Then take action, because there can be no change without action.

We will be asking twenty-one vital questions over the next twenty-one days. Years ago, in high school, my favorite English teacher told me that it takes twenty-one days to make a new habit. I have no idea if that is true, but I have heard other people say the same thing. It is a good place to start. You need time to practice a new way of thinking. If you make it for twenty-one days, then you will have learned a new skill, and that is our goal.

People sometimes develop "tunnel vision" where their focus is 100% on the negative parts of a situation while ignoring the positives! Remember the example of my grandmother who took everything and made it negative? You are given negative statements or you create them and then you believe it.

If you tell yourself a lie often enough it can become your new truth. If you dwell on the bad you will see more of it. Many people BELIEVE the negative self-talk because they have always believed it. It is a vicious cycle of self-fulfilling negativity.

People end up thinking negative thoughts all day by using that "tunnel vision" and focusing on the bad. You might not even realize you are doing it. The only way to change is to become more aware of what you are thinking. It is all about awareness and choices. The choices you make, make all the difference!

We are going to spend the time thinking about the way we think, how we think and what we think about. At the end of the twenty-one questions, we will take all that new awareness you have been creating and make positive changes. If your thinking is not helping you then it is time to create some new thoughts. This is not easy. But you can do it! I promise. You really can. It takes self-awareness and self-control.

The moment you make even just one minor change in your thinking, from negative to positive, you will begin feeling better. Even if you do this for just one day, instead of the full twenty-one days, there will be progress in your life. Slight changes add up until there are substantial changes! You will start the process of changing your thinking and reducing your stress.

Here is how this will happen: each day, for the next three weeks, you will take one set of questions a day and focus on that day's theme! You will do this by choosing a time each day to set aside a few minutes. If you are doing the "Attitude Adjustment" exercise in the mornings, then I would recommend that you do this work later on in the day. Or take ten minutes out of your lunch break. Anytime will work as long as you make a commitment.

When you read your daily questions, it will activate what I like to describe as the "Mini-Me Assistant" in the subconscious mind. Think of a mini version of you sitting at a little desk in your brain. This imagery of yourself as your own "Mini-Me Assistant" (MMA) sitting at a little desk is just a tool to help you access areas of your mind that might be a bit dusty from lack of usage. You are going to ask for help and she is going to rummage around in your mind and produce solutions!

Just know that all the images, thoughts, feelings, and experiences you have ever had are stored away somewhere in your mind. This is a variation of the Memory Palace that I explained earlier. But far more than just memories are available to you. All the creativity of the universe is at your disposal! You have the most complex piece of machinery ever created inside your skull cavity. USE IT! You just need help to process questions and get answers. That is the role of the MMA. Your "Mini-Me Assistant" will wander around in your brain, go into different areas of your mind, or rooms in your memory palace, and look for ideas and bits and pieces that she can synthesize into the beginning of an answer.

When you ask your MMA to help you understand where a negative idea comes from, she will bring you the answer. When you ask for a solution to a problem, she will work out a solution. The MMA will not be able to instantly answer all your questions or give you a solution in ten seconds. When negative thoughts and issues have been building for twenty years or more do not be surprised if it takes time to get an answer or a solution! That is why we will work on one theme for each day. We do not want to overwhelm the MMA.

This is a series of deeply personal questions. It will take some time to uncover your deepest fears and deepest wants. But once you find them, then you can work on them.

Each day you will write that day's questions down in a notebook. Writing each day is a crucial step! Do not skip it. When you put the pen to the paper, it is a permanent mark, a declaration of intent. When you finish writing the questions put the pen down. Close your eyes. Breathe deeply in and out several times like you did in meditation practice. Then imagine the MMA in your mind. Repeat the questions in your mind. Tell her that you want a solution, you want to find answers, and you want to make your life better. You will write down the ideas and images that come into your mind. That is the beginning of the answer.

Now, there are several ways that the answer can come. Some people will start writing at once after asking the questions because ideas will come quickly. Some will need to sit in silence until an idea/answer begins forming in their mind. If you do need to sit for several minutes, then just breathe deeply in and out like you do in meditation. The answers will come. Just give it some time.

Some people will need to write the questions down, activate the MMA, and then walk away for several hours. If you need to, then split this exercise up each day into two parts – the questions and the answers. You could write down the questions in your notebook at your lunch break, ask the MMA to help you, and then go do something else entirely. Go on and finish your work or run your errands.

At some point in your day, ideas, memories and images will begin to pop into your mind. From there, the answers will begin to form. Whatever the MMA brings to you, when those ideas pop into your head, just write it down in your notebook later. That is the beauty of your mind! Inspiration can come to you when you are not consciously thinking about it.

It all depends on how your mind works. One of these techniques will work for you – either sit and listen, start writing, or just go on with your day until the answer comes to you. Experiment and see which one works best.

Just one final bit of encouragement. Life is short. Each year only has 365 days. How quickly have they flown by already? How many years do you have left? Do you want the final years and days you have on this planet to be filled with hope and joy? Then make it so. You can do this. And if you miss a day just come back to it. Do not think you are a failure if this seems difficult. Many important things are.

READY? At this point, you will have chosen the time and the way you want to do this work. So, get your notebook prepared. Write a #1 on the first page, and then write the numbers 2-21 on the following pages.

Each day at your chosen time, write down the questions for that day AND the answers that come to you. Each day is going to bring you some new inspiration. Do not rush it. Take the time to fully explore your mind and your motivations. Focus on each day and each image or idea that comes your way.

If for some reason, a different question or set of questions comes to you after reading the questions I have prepared, then answer those questions instead! Your mind and spirit will lead you where it needs to go, so trust, follow and learn to answer those questions, too.

21 Days of Questions that can Change Your Life!

1. What gives my life meaning right now? What makes me happy? What makes me stressed out or depressed? (Make two lists.)

2. What makes me feel the most alive? What makes me most excited about living a good life? Or am I focused instead on just paying the bills instead of living a full and happy life?

3. What have been the most defining moments in my life that have helped shape who I am? How have I become me?

4. What did I dream about as a child? Did I have a goal or something that I loved when I was little that I

never got to do? What stopped me then? Can I do it now?

5. What life advice would I give my younger self? What life advice would I want to hear as an adult right now? Who do I listen to and why?

6. Am I living life according to the dreams, ideas, and expectations of someone else? If so, then why? And who are they? Or am I designing my own life?

7. What kinds of recurring situations do I seem to find myself in? Or what kind of people keep showing up in my life? Are they negative influences or positive? What kind of lessons have they taught me about myself?

8. What lies am I currently telling myself and others about who I am and about what is important to me? (Be honest with yourself right now. This is for your eyes only. No one else will see this.)

9. How would I describe myself to someone else? (Think beyond religion and politics please.) What are my best qualities? And what are my worst?

10. Do I avoid certain types of situations or people? What does that say about my life experiences and my beliefs or fears? Who or what do I avoid and why?

11. What is the most courageous thing I have ever done? How did I feel in that moment of time? Is there some situation right now where I am showing courage?

12. What is my worst fear? How does it limit my possibilities in life? What actions can I take to reduce my fears and believe in my ability to handle it?

13. What is the difference in the way I present myself to people around me and who I really am? What or who am I when no one else is around or watching?

14. Is there someone in my life that is stopping me from having a more fulfilling life? Who are they and how are they holding me back?

15. What hobbies or interests have I had in the last few years that intrigue me? What would I do if I had enough time? What do I do now when I have time for it?

16. What would my ideal day look like? What if I was doing what I love most to do and woke up every day feeling positive? How would that change my life?

17. Is there something I need to let go of to be able to move on with my life? What is the worst thing that could happen if I let go of the things that are no longer helping me? Can I let it go?

18. Why do I put off doing the things that make me happy and that I want to do? How can I show myself some love today? (Find at least one happy thing to do today!)

19. If there was just one life achievement that would make me feel proud of myself what would it be? What can I do today to move closer to that dream achievement?

20. If this was my last day alive, would I be satisfied with my life? What do I want my family to remember about me? Pick at least three things.

21. How many of the limited days I have left on this planet am I willing to waste being unhappy or dissatisfied with any part of my life?

YOU DID IT! You made it through twenty-one days of tough questions. I want you to go back and look through your notebook at those questions and answers. The answers will guide you in creating a happier, more fulfilled life. How? Now we get to define your goals, create more meaning, and continue to reduce the stress in your life!

I am very proud of you for taking the time to learn and practice. I am proud of you even if you didn't make it the whole twenty-one days. WHY? Because your intent is the most vital part of creating the change you want and need. There is no such thing as failure here.

Every step you make in the direction of peace, love and understanding is a good step. Just trying something positive and new is a step in the right direction. Even if you only made it through one day of the twenty-one questions, I want you to know that is enough to make a start. If you made it one day, then you can make it two. You are worth it. Just do not ever give up.

CHAPTER THEMES:
Choices and Action
21 Days of Vital Questions
Tunnel Vision
Mini-Me Assistant (MMA)
One Single Step

CHAPTER 18:
FIVE FACETS OF A HAPPY LIFE

"If you are not watching where you are going, then you just might end up where you do not want to be! Do not live life on autopilot."

THIS IS A FAST-PACED WORLD. It is a technology-driven world. Our children and grand-children are becoming addicted to ten-second sound bites and instant answers from search engines. Information is everywhere. Commercials are everywhere. It can be overwhelming. Even though the world is moving fast, there are plenty of reasons to slow it down.

So how do you create a new goal, change your life and reduce stress? First, realize that even though the world is fast-paced and instant, positive changes in life are not. This will take effort and time. But it will be worth it.

Just for a moment, think about the word time. In the larger world around us there is no time, there is no beginning or end. The Earth we live on, the Solar System, and the Universe have all existed before humans and will exist when humans are gone. Time means nothing in the bigger picture.

Our little moment of existence on this planet is like a flash and then it is gone. None of the fancy trappings of life are worth ruining your body and mind with stress, anxiety, and depression. And yet I still want pleasant things and a good life. I am sure that you do too. Where is the balance?

Everyone has a choice to make about how you spend your limited time in life. We are going to step back, away from the fast pace and create a life full of meaning. There is always something that you can change to make your life better. Even a few minor changes can reduce your stress, create more peace and a better life.

We are going to focus on several areas of life where you can create more meaning and make better choices. These are aspects of life that most people would consider important. We are going to start thinking about what makes life good, and then we are going to make it happen! Here are the areas we will focus on:

1. Family and Relationships
2. Career and Money
3. Lifestyle and Fun
4. Physical Health
5. Mental Health

As we focus on each of these five areas, we will be answering some basic questions about each one. The goal here is for you to further define the areas of your life that you choose to focus and work on. You might need much more work on one area than another. As you answer some basic questions about each area, you will find those issues where you can create more meaning and significance. Any obstacle is really an opportunity. These questions are just a beginning point. You might find an issue to work on that is not one of my listed questions. That is great!

Go grab your notebook again. In the last chapter you learned how to spend time thinking deeply about important questions. Now you will continue that work. You have trained your mind over the last twenty-one days to think deeply, access your universal creativity, and use the MMA to help find answers.

In this chapter the questions are just as important. But the timeframe is quite different! This will take about an hour to read through all the questions and find your areas that need work. This is great work for a weekend at home. Make a cup of tea, grab a snack, and get ready. These questions are broad and created to get you thinking about the major areas of life.

You will not need to work on every question. The goal is to find the areas that DO need work! Identifying the issues is a fabulous starting point. Change can only happen when you know what needs work. Get ready to write a statement about each issue that you would like to see changed. Then the fun begins in the next chapter as we create the scaffolding for actual change.

#1: FAMILY/RELATIONSHIPS

Are you satisfied with your family relationships?

Are you close to your parents/siblings?

Are your family relationships supportive?

Are you close to your children?

Are those relationships healthy?

Do you have conflict in your family right now?

Do you have close friendships?

Do you have a network of people to rely on?

Do you have good relationships with your neighbors?

Do you have romance in your life?

How is your relationship with your spouse?

Do you have a satisfying physical relationship?

Do you have trouble meeting new people?

Do you consider yourself a shy person?

Now you have found one or more

Family/Relationship issues that need work, so write

out a simple statement about what it is that you would

like to change.

#2: CAREER AND MONEY

How important is your career to you?

What if you could do other work for the same money?

Do you look forward to going to work each day?

Do you get recognition at work for what you contribute?

Do you work in a supportive and positive place?

Do you make enough money to meet monthly needs?

Are you able to give financially to other people?

Do you worry about your finances?

Do you have enough money for retirement?

Are you frightened by the idea of being poor?

Do you want to have money for helping your children?

Are you able to take care of your monthly expenses?

Do you believe that money is evil?

Do you have a will and life-insurance?

Now you have found one or more Career/Money issues that need work, so write a simple statement about what you would like to change.

_____

#3: LIFESTYLE AND FUN

Do you volunteer anywhere?

Do you routinely make a positive impact on people?

Do you encourage and support those around you?

Do you contribute to society with your time/money?

Do you have a hobby?

How important is having lots of free time?

Do you have activities that you enjoy?

Where would you like to go on vacation?

Do you play any sports?

Do you read for fun?

What was the last thing you read?

Do you routinely attend church services?

Do you have a fear of travel or flying?

Do you complain about your life?

Now you have found one or more Lifestyle/Fun issues that need work, so write a simple statement about what you would like to change.

#4: PHYSICAL HEALTH

How important is your physical health to you?

Would you consider yourself physically fit?

Do you drink alcohol to excess?

Do you use illegal drugs?

Do you need stimulants like coffee to function?

Do you have a routine sleep schedule?

Do you eat a lot of fast food?

Do you take vitamins or supplements?

Do you worry about your physical appearance?

Do you have a lot of stress in your life?

Are you comfortable with your physical appearance?

Are you able to physically move without discomfort?

Do you have a lack of energy?

Do you set a healthy example for your children?

Now you have found one or more Physical Health issues that need work, so write a simple statement about what you would like to change.

#5: MENTAL HEALTH

How mentally healthy do you feel right now?

Do you suffer with depression or anxiety right now?

Are you secure in who you are?

Do you love yourself?

Do you have safe boundaries with others?

Are you comfortable with how your life is right now?

Do you have difficulty expressing yourself when angry?

Do you often experience rage or anger?

Do you suffer from nightmares or panic attacks?

Do you have good self-control?

Do you have a positive or negative attitude?

Do you feel spiritually/emotionally strong?

Do you feel like your emotions are often out of control?

Do you often imagine bad things happening?

Do you spend time developing your spiritual side?

Now you have found one or more Mental Health issues that need work, so write a simple statement about what you would like to change.

CHAPTER THEMES:

Time is Limited

Identify the Issues

Five Areas to Discover

Creating Balance

CHAPTER 19: SMART GOALS AND DREAM BOARDS

"Dream again. You once were a child with big dreams. It is time to remember!"

NOW, WE WILL WRITE SMART goals for each of the identified issues from the last chapter. A SMART goal is: Specific, Measurable, Assignable, Realistic, and Time-Related. The first use of the term "smart" goals was by George Doran, in the November 1981 issue of *Management Review*. The idea of creating smart goals was first a tool used in business to boost productivity.

You can create smart goals for any (and all) of the personal issues that you want to work on. To help you understand the process, I will show you an example of one of my goals. You will see that this was a short-term goal, and I accomplished it in just one weekend. But I have used this exact same goal several times to wrap my hubby around my little finger. He cannot resist me when I am being so darn sweet. And then he just returns the favor. It is a win-win situation.

I found a Family/Relationship issue that needed work. I wanted to make my relationship with my husband stronger and happier. We often get so busy with work, that we forget to enjoy life. So, I wrote a simple statement about what I wanted to see change. Then, I produced a plan to achieve it.

This is my actual stated goal: "*I want to have a better relationship with my husband.*" That is a broad goal. I broke it down into a plan. Here is a template and my actual SMART plan for making it happen.

GOAL:_____

SPECIFIC: _____

MEASURABLE: _____

ASSIGNABLE: _____

REALISTIC: _____

TIME-RELATED: _____

Specific – The first step to making a goal possible is to make it specific. Define exactly what it is you want to achieve. Big goals can often be broken up into several small goals. In my example I want to feel closer to my husband. That is a big goal that I will make smaller by focusing on one single, specific way to make him happy and fulfilled this week.

Measurable - To make the goal measurable, you make it something that is defined. It could be measured in time, in volume, in weight, in output. Just make sure you have a clear sense of what success and completion will look like. I will accomplish my goal by spending more time with him in an activity of his choosing. I will ask him what he would like to do, and then do it with him.

Assignable (Action Steps)– Any goal you set must be something that can be assigned to someone on the team. It is totally easy when the team is just one person. (Remember that this was first a template for business teams.) For my needs, I change the A in SMART to "Action Steps." My goal will work because he wants to see that new movie and he loves popcorn.

Realistic – This goal is realistic because it is something that I can accomplish with my husband, and it is related to my over-all goal of having a happy relationship. I took that large goal and broke it down into this smaller step. Even though I do not love superhero movies, I can handle 2 hours watching some action movie he chooses. I will not eat my hubby's popcorn! That will make him even happier.

Time-Related – A goal with a short timeframe will keep you more motivated. My relationship goal will be accomplished this weekend. I will surprise him with the suggestion and keep back $20 for popcorn and candy.

One quick note here about having long-term goals. One-year or even five-year goals are huge targets that you plan for, like getting a college degree or saving for the down-payment on a house. The SMART goal template can help with both. You will probably find that many of your short-term goals are just part of the big picture of your long-term ones.

With a complex goal, I find it helpful to get a large piece of poster board and diagram or chart it all out. You can make a simple flow chart with a large goal at the top, then break the steps to reach that goal into individual smaller goals. Just make sure to write out each element of the long-term goal and break it into smaller actionable steps.

You will soon be on your way to creating a life of less stress and more significance. Please remember to be kind to yourself as you try to make changes. A realistic goal will be easier to achieve. And please take it slowly. Work on one change at a time. Do not stress yourself out. Setting goals like this is an act of LOVE for yourself! So be kind.

Focusing on your action is great, and that is what goal-setting is all about. But focusing on your thoughts is even better. Because thinking positive thoughts about your goals, will create even more positive thoughts and that will create more positive action. So how do you think positively about goal-setting? How about a Dream Board?

As we finish this section on the five facets of a happy life, I want to tell you about one of my favorite goal-setting projects. This is a fabulous way to learn to dream again. Children are great at having big plans and dreams. They will tell you about all the wonderful things that they are going to do when they grow up! But once we grow up, we forget our dreams. As adults, we need to learn to dream again.

If you need inspiration for goals in your life, then make a Dream Board. We are talking about waking dreams, or using your imagination in the daytime. Once you make a Dream Board, then you can also use it to fuel your nighttime dreams! More about that in just a minute.

In our bedroom, my husband and I created this simple way to keep our goals and dreams right in front of us. It is easy to get distracted and so busy that you forget what you are living and working for.

A Dream Board allows you to keep those ideals, those dreams you have for your life, right in front of you. Many people include things like a nice car or home on their Dream Board. And that is great because getting stuff is fun. But there is more to life than just accumulating stuff. Nothing that you own now will be yours forever. So go beyond the materialistic focus of getting more stuff. Get creative about what you want out of life and start dreaming again.

Let's say that you wanted to be a movie star when you were little. Well, you can still be involved in the arts. Find a theatre group to join or a bell choir or volunteer with your local high school drama department! Or maybe you wanted to be the President. Well, you can still be a part of government now. There are all sorts of regulatory, community boards that need more volunteers. And if you ever wanted to start a small business, well, there are Small Business Administration (SBA) groups in every state and they offer free planning assistance to small businesses! There is ALWAYS a way to reach for a dream.

To make my dream board, I went to a dollar store and bought a thick poster board. I also found some little decorations for it and got markers and sharpies. I had plenty of magazines lying around, so I started cutting pictures out of them. It is easy to find pictures of dream homes and fancy cars on the internet to print off. Finding a picture that represents "health" or "happiness" may be a bit more challenging. But that is also part of the fun of making a Dream Board. Get creative. We have a boat and travel destinations on there. I also have some pictures of jewelry, because I like the bling! And if you cannot find the perfect picture, well then find a phrase or saying that helps. I have some poetry and phrases on my half of the Dream Board.

Glue all the pictures on your poster board, decorate it all up, and there you have it. It is a fabulous way for you to remember just what you are living for. Many people will talk about what they would die for, but I am interested in what you will live for! Put the Dream Board somewhere so you will see it each day. Your dreams belong to you, so keep it private. Do not ever let anyone diminish or steal your dreams.

When you go to bed each night, look at the Dream Board and think of what each picture means to you, think of what it would mean to accomplish that goal.

Go to bed and imagine yourself with that goal already accomplished! See it, dream it and believe it. When you align your waking and sleeping thoughts on your dreams, then your actions will align, too.

CHAPTER THEMES:

S.M.A.R.T. Goals

Goal Setting as an Act of Love

Dream Boards

Go Beyond the Materialistic

Waking/Sleeping Dreams

CHAPTER 20: NEGATIVE PEOPLE, ANCHORS AND FORGIVENESS

"Protect your spirit from contamination. The less you deal with grumpy people, the happier your life will be."

IN THIS CHAPTER WE WILL be dealing with the negative people in our lives. I have three tips for you. The first is about perspective and the second is about creating anchors that take you mentally away from the negativity. Then finally, we will talk about forgiveness.

Stepping back from a situation and getting a new perspective can help you understand and process any situation. There are three positions of awareness to gain a new perspective about any issue you are facing. The goal is to look at and think about any difficult situation from each of these three different perspectives:

YOURSELF, The OTHER, and The OBSERVER.

I learned this technique back in my debate days in high school. In debate, you cannot defend your position fully unless you know the opposite position just as well as your own. You must learn to see all sides of an argument or idea.

We can get hyper-focused on our own perceptions. This happens often with stressful situations. Of course, you are going to feel the pain more if it happened directly to you! When someone is violent and destructive to others, then they are disconnected as humans to humanity as a whole.

They have lost their humanity. And it causes them personal pain which they spread to others. (Think of all the governments of the world who are involved in violence and destruction to others. It is not just an individual human problem; it is a problem of humanity as a whole.)

It helps to understand your pain when you can step back and look at it from another perspective. It has taken me a lot of practice to be able to step back and look at my situations from someone else's perspective. Think about a difficult situation you have experienced. What did you see? What did you hear? How are you feeling? This is all from your personal perspective.

Now step back and think about the same situation from another person's perspective. That person might feel radically different about the situation than you do. If they received no harm from the situation then they may have little compassion for any harm you received. If they are no accustomed to thinking of others, if they are self-centered, then they have no care or concern for your suffering. They are disconnected.

Now step back even further. Become a neutral observer. This perspective removes the cloud of emotions and looks instead just at facts. Your perspective, especially if you were the victim, will be different than the perspective of the perpetrator and different from the perspective of an observer. If you were a victim of a crime, then you suffered tremendously. To the criminal you were just another person to use and abuse. The criminal is more worried that they got caught. To the police officer who took your statement it was all another day on the job. They see so much violence because it is a part of their normal job experience.

Each person's reaction will be from their perspective: either YOURSELF, the OTHER, or the OBSERVER! This allows you to understand another person's viewpoint from their perspective and not just your own. Looking at your experiences from these other perspectives can be hard when you have so many emotions tied up in the experience. But this can also be beneficial to help with the healing process.

This technique of seeing a situation from someone else's perspective can also help you develop more compassion. This will help you deal with family who might not be supportive of what you are going through. Step back and look at it from their perspective. Do not look at them with anger. Look at them with eyes of understanding and wonder. Do not blame them for not knowing better. They may be stuck in their own conditioned way of thinking and blaming.

Often, if the people around you have not experienced the same stressful situations like you have, they might not have any way to really understand it. Your hard-headed family member has never developed the ability to get a new perspective. Now you get the chance to enlighten them. Just be kind! And do not be surprised if they do not listen or do not understand. No one changes unless their heart is open to change. No one listens unless their ears are open to hear.

When you have a negative experience, your mind and body can "remember" how you felt in that moment. This may be why some people have flashbacks and nightmares from their stressful experiences. It is like a little anchor from the past that can drag you in an instant all the way back to that moment in time. Think of your life experiences as if you are in a little sailboat. If the anchor is dropped, then it does not matter how much the wind blows, you will not be able to move forward. Bad feelings, smells, sights, sounds – can all be locked and stored in your memory. They can be anchors to your past experiences, your past traumas, your past stresses.

That emotional anchor can instantly transport you to the swamp of emotional pain. I do not like it when someone walks up behind me, even if it is my husband coming to put his arms around me. That motion of someone behind me is a trigger, an anchor, for feeling anxiety. That is how that first rapist attacked me.

If you have ever had a car wreck, then you know exactly what I mean. You might be fine driving down the road, until you come to THAT intersection or THAT spot where it occurred. Those bad feelings can show up each time you pass the place, or even when you just get in the vicinity of the intersection. That original experience becomes a negative trigger, a negative anchor.

I was one of the first on the scene when my friend Gina was in an awful wreck. She had just left my home. I always ask her to give me a call me when she gets back to her house. I did not hear from her, but from her husband. The wreck was just a few minutes from my home.

Thankfully, she was going to be okay physically. Those external scars healed, just like mine did after my three car wrecks. (Yes, three. And none of them were my fault.) But the internal, psychological and emotional scars were there, too. They were just invisible to others. But I knew they were there.

(Please always remember that everyone you meet has some inner pain, some invisible scars. Just always be kind and remember that.)

Gina recovered physically, but she needed help to recover emotionally. She would physically tighten up and the anxiety would ramp up when she got close to the intersection where the wreck happened. So, we made a plan to take that trigger and create a new anchor. I was driving, and prepared her for what was to come. I told her that we would be going through THAT intersection, but before we got to it, we were going to start shouting, at the top of our lungs, "I am alive! I am alive! I AM ALIVE!"

We must have looked like crazy women, laughing and yelling that phrase as loud as we could. But it made a difference. Now, every time she goes through THAT intersection, she focuses on the fact that she is alive. She does not feel the pain of the bad memories, instead, we took those bad memories and created better ones.

You can actively create a good anchor to minimize or even replace the bad. The whole point is to have something positive to focus your mind on that replaces the negative triggers and anchors. Feed your mind with whatever makes it stronger, happier and more resilient.

You might have a memory from your childhood of a wonderful smell that can take you right back to a happy place! Can you remember mom's cookies just warm from the oven when you got off the school bus? I can. Maybe the smell of a fresh-cut Christmas tree floods you with great memories of the holidays. Maybe a certain song always takes you right back to a happy dance in junior high or the first dance at your wedding. Those positive emotional memories are anchors that you can use to help you combat the negative anchors. When the bad memory tries to drag you to the swamp, actively replace it with a good memory.

Here are some more ideas about creating a positive anchor. Any of them will require a little bit of preparation. You can involve any of the five major senses – sight, smell, taste, hearing, touch.

If you know you will be dealing with a negative situation, then have a vial of some great essential oil nearby. Sniffing citrus, chocolate, or peppermint could help trigger a good feeling to replace or calm the bad. If there is a scent that reminds you of home, or love, or your grandma, then sniff it, and sniff it often when you are feeling stressed.

Or if you are in the car and you can turn on that one song that makes you happy, then turn it up! If you cannot turn up the radio, or you are in a place where you cannot make noise, then have a mantra prepared. A mantra can simply be a word or phrase that brings you comfort. (Just think of Gina and me going through that intersection yelling, "I AM ALIVE!") A verse from a holy book, a snippet of poetry, or a line from a song – all of these can be mantras that you can repeat to yourself. Use your mantra to replace the negative anchor with a positive one.

(To give your personal word, your mantra, even more power, use it during meditation! Get it associated with all the calm and happiness you feel when meditating!)

One last idea is to have a "lovey". Children often have their favorite toy, baby doll, or stuffed animal that makes them happy. You can have something like that, too. It can be something quite small that fits in your pocket, or it can be something larger that you carry in your purse or that sits on your desk. Make sure to create more than one. Use them often to help you when dealing with negative situations. You can use them when dealing with negative people.

The last tip for dealing with negative people deals with the issue of forgiveness. Forgiveness is a powerful emotion that could change your life. Many years ago, after I was raped in college, I chose to not focus on negativity and vengeance. I was originally willing to have him prosecuted. When the District Attorney told me to get therapy - because it was my word against the rapist - I took that advice. I am glad I did. It gave me a chance to begin to work on myself, my mind and spirit, my definitions of who and what I am. And over the years I found myself forgiving the rapist.

At one point, about 20 years ago, I began to worry about my decision to forgive. Was I weak? Was I too nice? Was I unconfrontational? Was I unbalanced? Was I just a total push-over? No, that is not it.

As I developed forgiveness for a rapist, I developed compassion for other people and situations in my life. If I was able to develop forgiveness for a violent criminal, then I could give forgiveness to the kind, but flawed people I am related to. I found myself filled with compassion for my siblings and my parents, for my first husband and his family. Instead of vengeance and negativity my goals became honesty and communication, first with myself and then with others around me.

In my heart I have forgiven all the people who have wronged me. It is not easy, especially with family. But I work on it consistently. Why? Because forgiveness makes me feel better. Forgiveness makes me a better person. NOT better than them, it does not make me better than the person I am forgiving. It makes ME a better person today than I was yesterday.

You might have heard the phrase, "being angry is like drinking poison and expecting your enemy to die." No one truly knows where this phrase comes from, but there are many variations. Why is it important to forgive? Because the anger in your heart is a poison that is far more damaging to you than it is to the other person. The anger in your heart can never touch them. All it can do is poison your heart, spirit, and mind.

Forgiveness is a sign of strength. It is a sign of maturity. It is a way to cut the ties, the anchors, the little connections that keep you linked to the evildoer, the perpetrator, the abuser. I do not forgive because it is good for them. I forgive because it is good for ME!

Forgiveness does not necessarily go hand-in-hand with forgetting. Those two get put together frequently. Instead, do not forget. Instead, remember and learn from the past. Learn from the awful people who hurt you. Learn why you do not want to be them. Never forget what your experiences taught you. Forgiveness frees you and allows you to move on!

Just a final thought here about negative people and situations – sometimes you cannot get away from them. The biggest negative in your life might be a parent, sibling, or situation that you cannot change for one reason or another.

In these situations, it is even more important that you guard your spirit from getting contaminated by the negativity. First, do not share all your happy thoughts and plans with negative people. You will never change them. They can only change themselves. And they will never do that unless they make that choice. They will not understand you, and they will not appreciate your words and your intent. Some things should just stay private in your head and heart.

Try to limit your exposure to the toxic people and situations in your life. Stop responding to negative talk. I had a family member who always wanted to remind me of something stupid I had done when I was a teenager. It would be brought up at family get-togethers and used as a weapon to hurt me. Guess what? I ignored it. I consistently ignored it. And eventually the negativity stopped.

Negativity grows and thrives on difficult, hateful interactions. Make it a point to send back love when they send you hate. If that seems impossible, then think of your interactions with them as a time for learning. Maybe you have learned from their example about who you do not want to be like, about how you do not want to live your life. Maybe you have grown stronger because of the struggle. Maybe you have grown more capable and more loving because of their negative example. Try to take a new look at the mean people in your life. Learn from them, send them back love, ignore negative words and attitudes, and just walk away when you can. You can love and respect someone by keeping them in your heart and mind, but you do not have to keep them in your life.

CHAPTER THEMES:

New Perspectives

Yourself, The Other, The Observer

5 Senses for Anchors

Essential Oils

Mantras

Forgiveness as a Super Power

CHAPTER 21: FINAL THOUGHTS

"Dear past, thank you for all the lessons. Because of you I am stronger and more resilient than I ever knew I could be. Dear future, I am ready!"

HERE WE ARE IN THE FINAL CHAPTER. But this can be another beginning instead. I want you to take every bit of this book to heart and let it inspire you. You really can change your life, reduce your stress, and move on!

The best part about making your own life better is that it spreads out from just you. Think of it like a little pebble thrown into a still pond. The ripples keep spreading out. The waves keep going all the way to the shore. You will be just like that little pebble. So please, do not minimize your small, positive actions. They may be small, but they can be mighty. Even one tiny action can make a difference. The changes you make in your life can ripple out and impact people you have not even met, or positively change the lives of your children and grandchildren.

Remember, this is our goal! You CAN take the worst that life gives you and turn it into something positive through your attitude and your choices. You can become happier, less stressed-out, more capable, and more loving.

I have always told my son that life will sometimes bring good results from bad decisions and bad results from good ones. Just always make the best decision that you can, knowing that it may not always go the way you think it should. Sometimes life brings tragic events and you do not get a choice at all. Life brought me molestation, rape, being disowned, betrayed and abandoned. It brought mental illness, car wrecks, life-threatening physical illness to my child, and the death of my spouse. Those are choices that life made for me!

What choices did life make for you? No one chooses cancer, or debilitating disease, losing their home, or losing their job, the color of their skin, or their genetics, their sexual orientation or even the country in which they are born. There is so much that we cannot control.

You DO get to choose how to respond to what life gives you. That is where you have control. That is where you stand in the position of power. In the position of love, and acceptance. In the position of peace and happiness. Between action and reaction, there is a pause. In that little moment of eternity, take a deep breath, because you get to make that choice. That moment is yours. It is up to you!

I have found that the more we understand all the things we have in common the less our differences matter. As you look around at the people in your life remember that each one of them has a private pain. Each one of them has a private hurt they are struggling with. When you figure this out you will find the wellspring of compassion inside you.

I like helping people find that compassion, for themselves and for others. It is an amazing thing to be able to help someone heal their own wounds. Through classes and retreats, I get the chance to know more people and hear their stories. I would love to hear yours. If you are interested in classes with me, where we go deeper into the subject of transformation, then send me an email.

Each year my team and I plan small, exclusive retreats with about 20 people. We go through many subjects from this book and much, much more. If you are interested in coming to the USA's heartland and communing with me and my team on a camping retreat, then send me an email and let me know. We are booking for the next year's retreats right now. (COVID may have slowed us down, but we will be back to having real in-person retreats as soon as possible!)

If you would like ME to come to YOUR retreat, seminar, or workshop as a keynote speaker then I would love to do that. Just send me an email requesting more information about my speaker's fees and what is included. Please have an idea of the total number of attendees, the venue, and dates. I can even do video conferences online for distance workshops!

Every person who reads this book is now a part of a new group – a tribe of warrior/survivors filled with strength and compassion. Come visit my website and read my blog at: www.ShannaWarner.com. While there you can get the links for the Guided Meditations. You can also sign up for an email newsletter or send me a message. You can also find me on Facebook. Just look for: facebook.com/pages/whatshallwereadtoday. Come follow along and join my groups, and we will chat more about positive, uplifting ways to beat stress.

Okay, now get out there! Make your life better. Find what makes you satisfied and happy. I am so proud of you for just taking the time and effort to read this book. I know how hard it is to look deeply in the mirror of your own soul and not flinch. Making positive changes is hard. Is it worth it? Absolutely. Is it always easy? No way. And yet here you are! I look forward to hearing from you someday soon.

CHAPTER THEMES:

Each End is A Beginning

Pebble in a Pond

Control the Response

Contact Me

Retreats, Seminars, Workshops

BONUS #1:
MY READING LIST

"Some of my best friends are good books. They
have given me comfort and advice, and helped
cheer a gloomy day."

HERE IS MY PERSONAL TOP 10 list of
therapeutic/motivational books and why each of them
is in my personal library. I will tell you a little about
each book and then I would like to encourage you to
pick one and read it! Or go online to my website or
Facebook page and send me a message about the
books that YOU love the best and tell me why.

1. *The Road Less Traveled* - M. Scott Peck

2. *The Greatest Miracle in the World* -Og Mandino

3. *The Four Agreements* – Miguel Ruiz

4. *Make Your Bed* – Admiral William McRaven

5. *The Art of Mindfulness* – Thich Nhat Hanh

6. *The Power of Myth* – Joseph Campbell

7. *The Prophet* – Kahlil Gibran

8. *Proof of Heaven* – Eben Alexander

9. *Balcony People* – Joyce Heatherley

10. *The Lord of the Rings* – J.R.R. Tolkein

The Road Less Traveled - Scott Peck was a psychiatrist who was concerned about the spiritual development of his patients. He wrote about how to help people grow, linking psychology and spirituality. His discussions on love are brilliant and his ideas about divinity helped me understand my connection to the divine. This is my absolute favorite work of non-fiction. It profoundly changed my life and helped me survive through some terrible stress.

The Greatest Miracle in the World - Og Mandino's chapter that has the "Memo from God" is one of the most brilliant pieces of writing I have ever had the pleasure to read. While I do not agree with all the assertions he makes about the divine, it is a piece that will make you cry and believe again in your own self-worth. Your very life is a miracle - always remember that! This is a quick and easy read, and worth every moment.

The Four Agreements - Miguel Ruiz's work is a collection of wisdom in the philosophical tradition of the Toltecs. It will be quite a different book for people unused to reading philosophy. It is not easy to understand, but it is easy to read. It will be one of those books that you will have to spend time thinking about. And maybe read it a second time for all the information to sink in. There are incredibly powerful truths in four simple statements. Make it through that first chapter, and it will be smooth sailing from there.

Make Your Bed - The Admiral wrote a very charming book about his military training days. It was originally a speech he crafted as the keynote speaker for a graduation ceremony. He developed it into a book, and it is well worth your time to read. Whenever you need a quick pick-me-up, this is a great uplifting one. Each chapter tells a separate story, and all of them are inspirational. Get ready to gain a new appreciation for our armed forces. This book is a wonderful gift for young people.

The Art of Mindfulness – As one of the most revered teachers in the world, Thich Nhat Hanh explains why meditation matters. He teaches that by devoting 100% of our attention on what we are doing in the moment, we can alleviate suffering, fear, and anxiety. With mindfulness and the practice of looking deeply at our thoughts, we can transform and heal the problems in life. Even something in your day as simple as sitting to drink a cup of tea can become a mindful moment.

The Power of Myth - Joseph Campbell's study of myth and how it connects to our lives today is powerful. He is great at linking present lives to the past stories our great cultures are based on. So many people forget that our lives today have been shaped by the cultures of the past. His advice to "Follow Your Bliss" has always been one of my favorite ideas to share with people, young and old!

The Prophet - I have a pocket-sized *Prophet* by Kahlil Gibran that I carry with me often. I have used sections of this poetic book of wisdom at funerals and at weddings. It is written in small sections that deal with specific topics of life. The sections about children, parents, and death are some of the most powerful pieces in the book. They brought comfort to me on the days when my son was closest to death. And the sections on love and marriage were read at my wedding.

Proof of Heaven - Dr. Eben Alexander's book had a profound effect on me. It is hard to argue with a brilliant brain surgeon and his discussion of what happens to the brain in death. Especially when he is the one who nearly died and came back from the brink! And from a place he experienced as heaven, populated with family he did not even know existed - but who reached out to him on his journey. Amazing. His story deserves a read and a discussion, even from the people who do not, and never will, believe in an afterlife. Dr. Alexander did not believe either until he experienced it.

Balcony People – Joyce Heatherley's book is simple and small, perfect for an afternoon of peaceful reading on a rainy day. Expect to have your entire perspective changed. It certainly did that for me! She explains that in your personal world you need to find the people who are up on the balcony - those who want to lift you higher and higher to be with them. Go out there and find the people who make your life better. Accentuate the positive, eliminate the negative!

The Lord of the Rings - No book list is complete for me personally without Tolkien's LOTR. It has been, and always will be, my ideal of fiction perfection. I first read about the realm of the hobbits when I was a young girl. LOTR swept me away into a world filled with magic and mysticism, and the battle between good and evil. The simple hobbits are focused on enjoying life and yet they become heroes when the need arises. Even when all seems lost, the main characters continue to fight the battle and follow through with their heroic deeds. They are distinguished role models, even though they are imaginary.

BONUS #2:
100 POSITIVE AFFIRMATIONS

"Look inside for the strength and inspiration you need. It is really there, I promise you. Just dig deep and you will find it!"

I was made with divine intentions.

I will not sweat the small stuff. Everything is small stuff.

I will overcome my fears by following my dreams.

I can. I will. End of story.

I am in charge of how I feel. Today I choose happiness.

I will not compare myself to strangers on the Internet.

I am choosing and not waiting to be chosen.

I have the power to create change.

I will not quit; I will explore all possibilities.

I will choose to speak positive words.

I will not stop when I am tired, I will stop when I am done.

Success is my driving force.

The success of others will not make me jealous. My time will come.

I will speak with confidence.

I can say "No" when I need to.

The only person who can defeat me is myself.

I will be true to myself.

I choose to accept myself as I am.

Situations change, and I will be okay.

If I fail, I will fail while trying.

My confidence will grow as I grow.

Someone else's bad attitude is not my attitude.

Happiness is within my grasp.

I will keep working until it gets better.

I am a work in progress. It is okay to be me.

The tools I need to succeed are here inside me.

Happiness is inside me.

I choose hope over fear.

Positivity is my choice!

I will ignore gossip and negative talk.

I am a diamond. It is time for me to shine.

I will stop apologizing for being myself.

Negative self-talk has no place in my life.

I will work on my fears today.

I am grateful for the things I have.

I will achieve my goals.

My focus on success is unwavering.

My need is strong, so I will find a way.

I am committed to becoming the person I want to be.

Success is in my future.

I will keep my focus on my goals.

I am my own best chance for success.

I choose to be constantly improving.

I desire to learn new things.

It is not a challenge; it is an opportunity.

I have a growth mindset.

I will create joy in my life.

I will be proactive in removing obstacles.

My successes and my failures belong to me.

I am not dependent on anyone else.

I will follow my dreams.

The little things in life make all the difference.

I will find new positive friends.

My fear goes away as I live my life with courage.

I can go with the flow.

I am happy, healthy and centered.

Change is just another opportunity.

I am calm and in control of my emotions.

My strength is stronger than my fear.

I move beyond stress to peace.

My thoughts are positive and full of joy.

My life is an adventure.

Today I will let go of "what if" and focus on now.

Calm is my primary state of being.

I am unique and I am okay with that.

I will work smarter, not harder.

I am a positive influence.

I will choose to surround myself with positive people.

I feel free to give myself the TLC I need.

Positive energy surrounds me.

I am calm and confident.

New opportunities are coming my way.

I will attract positive people to me.

When opportunity knocks, I will be prepared to answer the door.

I have all the power I need to create the success I want.

The universe is sending positive opportunities to me.

I will not be distracted from my goals and vision.

Every day is filled with new ideas and possibilities.

I am open minded and willing to explore any path to success.

Negative beliefs have no power over me.

I am optimistic and open minded.

I control my thoughts; I will not let my thoughts control me.

My passion for helping others brings tangible results.

I will not let others impose their limitations on me.

I am fully committed to achieving success in my life.

My only limit is myself.

I am prepared for the challenges of the day.

Today I am filled with positive energy.

I choose to remain calm.

I will face this day with confidence and positivity.

I am energized by the thought of a new day.

My day is full of possibilities and potential.

My day is a blessing and a gift that I will not waste.

I trust my inner wisdom to guide me through my day.

I will not compare myself to others.

My day is full of opportunity and I will say yes.

I will face the day with an open heart and open mind.

Today I feel healthy and strong, physically, emotionally and mentally.

Today I will accomplish great things.

<u>I will make today AMAZING!</u>

ABOUT THE AUTHOR

Shanna Warner has a degree in Communications and English. She began her career in radio, worked in journalism, and at one point was a professional musician.

She and her husband currently publish a holistic health and wellness magazine in Oklahoma – *Natural Awakenings*. They also publish paperbacks, ebooks, audiobooks and a podcast through their publishing company Manna Services Group.

She is most proud of being a mom, and keeping her little son alive through all the horrors they faced. She is also proud to call herself a survivor, and wants every person who has been beaten down to know that they CAN rise!

Shanna is currently working on several projects, including a screenplay, more nonfiction, and two paranormal book series for young adults. She is the author of *"Stuck at Home: 125 Easy and Cheap Activities for Parents and Kids"* and *"Ghost Encounters: 13 True Tales of the Supernatural."*

Her websites and contact information are available in the Resources Section of this book.

RESOURCES

https://www.ShannaWarner.com - I recorded those three guided mediations, and they are free for anyone to listen to. They are available via a link to Anchor, where I also record my podcast. Just check out the website for instructions on how you can listen to them. You can join my email list when you visit the website, learn about new classes and retreats or read one of the blog posts. You can also find info about some of my other books. I look forward to meeting you! AND I will be your "Balcony Friend."

https://www.NAOklahoma.com - Natural Awakenings is a free magazine that my husband and I publish in Oklahoma. The printed magazine can be found in Oklahoma City and Tulsa. You can read the digital magazine on the website. The magazine is also represented on Facebook, Instagram, Pinterest and Twitter.

https://anchor.fm/natural-awakenings – Along with the magazine, we have a Mind-Body-Spirit podcast titled "Natural Awakenings." You can find it wherever you listen to podcasts, like Spotify or iTunes.

https://www.ChildSafeCleaners.com – Go here to get more information about healthy alternatives to harsh chemicals. I partnered with a manufacturing company here in the USA that is all about health and wellness. Getting rid of household chemicals that can make asthma worse for kids is part of my focus!

https://www.WorkFromHomeAndLoveIt.com – Go there to find out about working with me, and two of my closest friends. We are very much into environmental issues, health and wellness, and safer household products. We believe in healthier choices for a healthier life and planet.

On Facebook, my writer's page – "Once Upon A Book" www.facebook.com/WhatShallWeReadToday. There is a group there focused on stress reduction. That group is for anyone, male or female, who has big stress in their life, maybe have gone through trauma, or for partners of survivors to learn more. It is also available as another support system for the people who are in private study with me through classes and seminars!

On Facebook - Look for: "Success With Shanna and Mark"–facebook.com/PlanTodayReapTomorrow. This is our business Mastermind group. Join our group if you are interested in knowing more about how I run my magazine, my life as a writer, a business coach, and in my health and wellness business. I am a fan of Napoleon Hill's writings, so you will probably see a post about that! If you like what you have learned and are interested in working with me in a business setting, then please visit one of my websites. My hubby and I own several businesses, and all of them are about helping people! I mentor and train people every week.

www.adaa.org - The Anxiety and Depression Association of America – more fabulous information that can help you right now.

www.VA.gov - Our USA Veteran's Affairs Department has fabulous information about PTSD in their health section. It has information for everyone, not just Veterans. Thank you to all our Veterans for their service!

www.PTSD.gov - Another government website that has great info about Post-Traumatic Stress Disorder.

http://orgs.utulsa.edu/trapt/errt/ Dr. Joanne Davis and her team at the University of Tulsa are leading the way in research and treatment for trauma victims. Please reach out to them if you are suffering with nightmares related to trauma.

https://beckinstitute.org/ Dr. Aaron Beck is the father of Cognitive Behavioral Therapy. He developed the AWARE method for dealing with panic and anxiety. Their website has all sort of great information about anxiety and depression that might help you. Clark, David J and Beck, Aaron T. (2012). "The Anxiety and Worry Workbook: The Cognitive Behavioral Solution" New York, The Guilford Press.

https://www.projectsmart.co.uk/brief-history-of-smart-goals.php A brief history of SMART goals.

Doran, G.T. (1981). "There's a S.M.A.R.T. Way to Write Management's Goals and Objectives", Management Review, Vol. 70, Issue 11, pp. 35-36.

Amy Cuddy's TED talk:

https://www.ted.com/talks/amy_cuddy_your_body_l anguage_may_shape_who_you_are?language=en

When you listen to the guided meditations on my podcast, all the music was created by composer Kevin MacLeod. You can find more of his music at InCompeTech.com.

For "The 10-Minute Power Nap" Guided Meditation

"Ever Mindful" Kevin MacLeod (incompetech.com)

Licensed under Creative Commons: By Attribution 3.0 License

http://creativecommons.org/licenses/by/3.0/

For "Your Secret Hideaway" Guided Meditation

"Fluidscape" Kevin MacLeod (incompetech.com)

Licensed under Creative Commons: By Attribution

THE END

(But it's really just another beginning!)

www.ingramcontent.com/pod-product-compliance
Lightning Source LLC
Chambersburg PA
CBHW051821040426
42447CB00006B/303